SpringerBriefs in Law

More information about this series at http://www.springer.com/series/10164

Steven Brian Gallagher

Protecting Built Heritage in Hong Kong

Springer

Steven Brian Gallagher
Faculty of Law
Chinese University of Hong Kong
Shatin, Hong Kong

ISSN 2192-855X ISSN 2192-8568 (electronic)
SpringerBriefs in Law
ISBN 978-981-16-5070-3 ISBN 978-981-16-5071-0 (eBook)
https://doi.org/10.1007/978-981-16-5071-0

© The Author(s), under exclusive license to Springer Nature Singapore Pte Ltd. 2021
This work is subject to copyright. All rights are solely and exclusively licensed by the Publisher, whether the whole or part of the material is concerned, specifically the rights of translation, reprinting, reuse of illustrations, recitation, broadcasting, reproduction on microfilms or in any other physical way, and transmission or information storage and retrieval, electronic adaptation, computer software, or by similar or dissimilar methodology now known or hereafter developed.
The use of general descriptive names, registered names, trademarks, service marks, etc. in this publication does not imply, even in the absence of a specific statement, that such names are exempt from the relevant protective laws and regulations and therefore free for general use.
The publisher, the authors and the editors are safe to assume that the advice and information in this book are believed to be true and accurate at the date of publication. Neither the publisher nor the authors or the editors give a warranty, expressed or implied, with respect to the material contained herein or for any errors or omissions that may have been made. The publisher remains neutral with regard to jurisdictional claims in published maps and institutional affiliations.

This Springer imprint is published by the registered company Springer Nature Singapore Pte Ltd.
The registered company address is: 152 Beach Road, #21-01/04 Gateway East, Singapore 189721, Singapore

Preface

Hong Kong is a modern vibrant city, characterised as a city of skyscrapers around the Victoria Harbour with little place for old buildings. However, Hong Kong still has a surprising number of buildings and sites that have cultural and historical significance. These include buildings and sites from its pre-colonial and colonial period (Hong Kong was a British colony between 1841 and 1997[1]). This book considers that built heritage and the problems that arise with protecting it in Hong Kong. These problems include the usual issues in achieving a balance between development and loss of built heritage in a dynamic city. For example, pressures of population, fashion, finance and politics driving development and redevelopment of its built landscape. A further complication for Hong Kong's built heritage preservation is its small reserve of developable land. Furthermore, Hong Kong has faced and still faces a unique problem in built heritage protection; it has long been considered a "borrowed place".

This book provides a history of the development of protection for built heritage in Hong Kong and considers different forms of protection that have been involved, including private, legal and popular protection. In particular, the book notes the problems built heritage has faced and is facing in Hong Kong and the importance of social unrest movements in developing the administrations' policies and legal protection for the built heritage of Hong Kong.

Among the book's conclusions are that protecting built heritage was not a major concern for the colonial administration and has not been a major concern for the post-handover administration in their plans for urban development. It also concludes that an important factor driving the policy of development of built heritage post-1997 was an attempt to distance Hong Kong from its colonial past. However, as the people of Hong Kong have seen their built heritage threatened and demolished, there has been more popular discontent voiced over this loss of heritage, increased questioning of government policy and, in particular, criticism of the fitness for purpose of the legal and regulatory regime intended to protect built heritage. The book concludes by

---

[1] The geographic extent of the colony changed during that period. Originally, the colony consisted of Hong Kong Island alone; Hong Kong extended with the inclusion part of the Kowloon Peninsula in 1860, and finally the rest of Kowloon and the new territories with the leasing of this area for 99 years in 1898. In 1997, the whole of Hong Kong ceased to be a British colony and became the Hong Kong Special Administrative Region (SAR) of the People's Republic of China.

considering the future for built heritage and its protection in Hong Kong, including how to improve the legal and regulatory framework to achieve a balance between the pressures on developable land in Hong Kong and maintaining built heritage.

Hong Kong Victoria Harbour at night (colour)

Shatin, Hong Kong   Steven Brian Gallagher

Contents

1	**Built Heritage in Hong Kong**	1
	1.1 Introduction—Why "Built Heritage"?	1
	1.2 What Built Heritage in Hong Kong?	4
	1.3 Problems for Built Heritage in Hong Kong	5
	1.3.1 Common Problems for Built Heritage in Hong Kong	6
	1.3.2 Particular Problems for Built Heritage in Hong Kong	7
	References	12
2	**The Development of Protection for Built Heritage in Hong Kong up to 1976**	15
	2.1 Introduction	15
	2.2 The Development of Protection for Built Heritage in Hong Kong	16
	2.3 The Beginnings of Built Heritage Protection in Hong Kong	18
	2.3.1 First Statutory Protection of Built Heritage in Hong Kong- Special Ordinances	19
	2.3.2 First Statutory Protection of Built Heritage in Hong Kong—General Ordinances	21
	2.4 The Second World War	24
	2.5 Continued Non-Legal Protection of Built Heritage in Hong Kong	26
	2.6 The Development of the Antiquities and Monuments Ordinance	27
	References	29
3	**The Antiquities and Monuments Ordinance (Cap. 53)**	33
	3.1 Introduction	33
	3.2 Built Heritage as "Antiquity" or Site Containing "Relics"	34
	3.3 Built Heritage as "Monument" or "Proposed Monument"	35
	3.3.1 Objection to Declaration as Monument or Proposed Monument	37
	3.3.2 Compensation for Declaration as Monument	38
	3.4 Antiquities and Monuments Office	39

	3.5	Antiquities Advisory Board (AAB)	40
	References		41
4	**Problems with the Antiquities and Monuments Ordinance Pre-1997**		43
	4.1	Introduction	43
	4.2	Hong Kong Heritage Society 1976–1984	44
	4.3	Monument Declarations to 1984	45
	4.4	Sino-British Joint Declaration of 1984	47
	4.5	Ohel Leah Synagogue 1985–89	47
	4.6	The New Territories in the 1980s and 1990s	49
	4.7	Declared Monuments in the Run-Up to "The Handover"	51
	4.8	The Last Colonial Built Heritage Issue-Victoria Harbour	51
	References		52
5	**The Hong Kong SAR and Built Heritage 1997–2006**		53
	5.1	Introduction	53
	5.2	Positive Signs for Built Heritage Protection	54
		5.2.1 The Urban Renewal Authority	54
		5.2.2 Civic Exchange "Saving Hong Kong's Heritage" Report, 2002	55
		5.2.3 The Second "Proposed Monument" Declaration: Morrison Building, 2003	56
		5.2.4 Proposed Development of Kom Tong Hall, 2002–4	57
		5.2.5 Antiquities and Monuments Office's Territory-Wide Survey of Historic Buildings	57
	5.3	Problems for Built Heritage Under the Post-Colonial Government	58
		5.3.1 Allegations of Corruption in the Antiquities and Monuments Office, 2002	58
		5.3.2 Continued Problems for Victoria Harbour	59
	5.4	Conclusion—1997–2006	60
	References		60
6	**Heritage and Social Unrest: 2006–7**		61
	6.1	Introduction	61
	6.2	Star Ferry and Queen's Pier	62
		6.2.1 Star Ferry 2006	63
		6.2.2 Queen's Pier 2007	63
	6.3	Wedding Card Street and the Urban Renewal Authority 2007	64
	6.4	King Yin Lei 2007	65
	6.5	Conclusion—2007	65
	References		66

7	**The Government's Heritage Concessions**		69
	7.1 Introduction		69
	7.2 The Secretary for Development-The Antiquities Authority		70
	7.3 Chief Executive's Policy Address 2007		70
		7.3.1 The Commissioner for Heritage's Office	71
		7.3.2 Heritage Impact Assessments	71
		7.3.3 Revitalizing Historic Buildings Through Partnership Scheme	73
		7.3.4 Economic Incentives and Financial Support to Owners of Historic Properties	74
	7.4 Intangible Cultural Heritage Policy		74
	7.5 Conclusions on the Government's Heritage Concessions		75
	References		75
8	**Hong Kong Built Heritage Failures and Successes Post-2007**		77
	8.1 Introduction		77
	8.2 Hong Kong Built Heritage Problems and Failures Post-2007		78
		8.2.1 World Heritage Site: 2012 Victoria Harbour or Chi Lin Nunnery?	78
		8.2.2 Heritage Impact Assessment Policy	79
	8.3 Hong Kong Built Heritage Positives and Successes Post-2007		80
		8.3.1 Marine Police Headquarters Compound– "1881 Heritage "or "Disney Heritage"?	80
		8.3.2 Urban Renewal Authority Since 2007	81
		8.3.3 Proposed Monument Declarations	84
		8.3.4 Consultation on Built Heritage Preservation	89
		8.3.5 Revitalizing Historic Buildings Through Partnership Scheme	90
		8.3.6 Declared Monuments	92
		8.3.7 The Antiquities Advisory Board Grading System	93
	8.4 Private Built Heritage Protection and Public Private Partnerships		98
	References		104
9	**Conclusions and The Future for Built Heritage Protection in Hong Kong**		109
	References		111

List of Figures

Fig. 1.1	Murray House, formerly in Central now in Stanley	11
Fig. 1.2	Sung Wong Toi as it is today	12
Fig. 2.1	Sai Kung Kindergarten	26
Fig. 3.1	Duddell Street granite steps and gas lamps	41
Fig. 6.1	King Yin Lei	66
Fig. 8.1	Heritage 1881	100
Fig. 8.2	Blue House Wan Chai (colour)	101
Fig. 8.3	Cenotaph	102
Fig. 8.4	Empire Theatre (State Theatre) North Point	103
Fig. 8.5	Pagoda Ping Shan trail	103
Fig. 8.6	Leung Yeuk Tau Trail	104

Chapter 1
Built Heritage in Hong Kong

Abstract A number of terms have been used to describe old buildings and archaeological and historical sites that should be protected for future generations. The term "Built Heritage" most appropriately identifies humankind's effects upon the natural landscape which should be protected as examples of humankind's activities and achievements and passed on to future generations. Surprisingly to many Hong Kong has a wealth of built heritage. This heritage faces the usual problems common to most modern cities, for example pressure of population growth and pollution, but also is threatened by some problems specific to Hong Kong—especially the identification of Hong Kong as a "borrowed" or temporary place.

1.1 Introduction—Why "Built Heritage"?

There are different terms which may be used to refer to evidence of humankind's effect on the natural landscape which are significant to a society. This book will use the term "built heritage", for a number of reasons. First, although other terms have been popular in the recent past they do not cover all examples of humankind's effect on the environment as clearly as the term built heritage. For example, the term "immoveable heritage", although linked to the lawyer's favoured term "immoveable property", is inappropriate for much built heritage today. This is because this term derives from property law, which separates real property (land and interest in land) from personal property (everything except land). In Hong Kong we define the terms "immoveable property" and "movable property" in our ordinances,[1] and have different legal rules for the treatment of both. Thus, the concept of immoveable, a fixture on the land, communicates that it forms part of the land and so is subject to the law affecting real property (land). This is in contrast to the concept of a "fitting" which is easily removed

---

[1] The concept of "immoveable property" is defined in s 3 of the Interpretation and General Clauses Ordinance (Cap 1) as: (a) land, whether covered by water or not; (b) any estate, right, interest or easement in or over any land; and (c) things attached to land or permanently fastened to anything attached to land. Moveable property is defined as property of every description except immovable property.

from a building and so constitutes "moveable" or personal property. However, not all buildings or other examples of man's impact on the landscape are immoveable. For example, Murray House, a building built in 1844 in Central, Hong Kong, as a part of the barracks for British soldiers, was dismantled in 1982 to make way for the new Bank of China Building. The pieces of Murray House were then transported to Stanley waterfront on the south side of the Island and rebuilt in 1999.[2] Thus the term "immoveable" is not entirely appropriate for all evidence of man's impact on the landscape.

Another term which has been popular is "built environment", which was used in the United Nations Educational, Scientific and Cultural Organization (UNESCO) Recommendation on the Historic Urban Landscape, 2011.[3] The term was identified as referring "to human-made (versus natural) resources and infrastructure designed to support human activity, such as buildings, roads, parks, and other amenities." The built environment may therefore encompass the natural environment in its creation, and the natural environment is often integral to the built environment, thus the two become part of the built environment: an example that illustrates this formation of the natural environment into the built environment in Hong Kong is the Victoria Harbour (sometimes referred to as "the Harbour" because of its importance to Hong Kong and because it is almost synonymous with Hong Kong- and not least because this avoids the embarrassment of associations with Hong Kong's colonial past.). Victoria Harbour is an example of built and natural environment which is an intrinsic part of Hong Kong's cultural heritage as a heritage landscape.

However, as we are discussing aspects of the built environment which have heritage value, in this section we will use the term "built heritage" because it reflects the wide variety of heritage which may be created by man's interaction with the environment and landscape and encompasses what may be considered minor alterations of the landscape as well as more major constructions. The term "cultural heritage" is a term of international law, derived from six international conventions.[4] However, as Hong Kong is not burdened by too much international law and is party to only two of these conventions,[5] the international law meaning has little significance. Further,

---

[2] South China Morning Post and Peters [15].

[3] UNESCO [22].

[4] The Convention for the Protection of Cultural Property in the Event of Armed Conflict, 1954; The Convention on the Means of Prohibiting and Preventing the Illicit Import, Export and Transfer of Ownership of Cultural Property, 1970; The Convention Concerning the Protection of the World Cultural and Natural Heritage, 1972.

The Convention on Stolen or Illegally Exported Cultural Objects, 1995; The Convention on the Protection of the Underwater Cultural Heritage, 2001; and, The Convention for the Safeguarding of the Intangible Cultural Heritage, 2003.

[5] The Convention Concerning the Protection of the World Cultural and Natural Heritage, 1972, and The Convention for the Safeguarding of the Intangible Cultural Heritage, 2003.

1.1 Introduction—Why "Built Heritage"?

as Hong Kong has reference to the term "cultural heritage" in only one of its ordinances,[6] and there only as a courtesy,[7] the term is used here in its more general and all-encompassing meaning rather than its international law specific meaning. Thus, in this text, "cultural heritage is evidence of the activities and achievements of humankind that should be passed on for the benefit of future generations."[8] From this general definition of cultural heritage we can identify built heritage as any evidence of the activities and achievements of humankind affecting the natural landscape and subsequent changes to these that should be passed on for the benefit of future generations.

The term "built heritage" therefore will be used to refer to traditional built structures, for example houses, flats, shops, temples and churches, forts and other military installations, piers and bridges. The term will also be used for changing of the landscape, for example reclamation of land from the seas, terracing of the land for cultivation, cultivation of the land, harbours, quarries, roads, bridges, paths and rock art-examples of all of these have been recognised as part of the cultural heritage of Hong Kong and many examples have been declared as monuments.[9] Thus, built heritage may range in scale from the monumental to the barely noticeable. For an example of the monumental we may consider again the Victoria Harbour. The development of the Victoria Harbour has been a monumental activity and achievement of the people of Hong Kong as they live on it, build around it, reclaim land from it and maintain it. As heritage, the Victoria Harbour is the reason for Hong Kong's existence and continuing success. For example of the relatively minor and easily missed built heritage, we may consider scratched designs on rocks in Sai Kung which evidence early occupation of Hong Kong,[10] or single stones placed in significant *Feng Shui* spots in indigenous villages in Hong Kong's New Territories, to mark respect points for earth gods.[11]

The term may also be used for landscapes themselves and the community within the landscape. The issue of community has become of more concern in Hong Kong in recent years, for example the Pok Fu Lam village has been suggested as a possible World Heritage Site, although there are few old buildings remaining.[12] Similarly, concerns have been raised about the redevelopment of many old buildings in Sham Shui Po both because of the loss of the buildings as built heritage themselves, and

---

[6] Environmental Impact Assessment Ordinance (Cap. 499), considered in Chap. 6.

[7] The term was also used in the tile of Hong Kong's government sponsored Consultation. Antiquities Advisory Board [1].

[8] Gallagher [3].

[9] Antiquities and Monuments Office Website [2].

[10] For example, the rock art inscriptions on Kau Sai Chau in Sai Kung which are a declared monument. AMO 2.

[11] In other jurisdictions another example of what might be considered a minor interaction with the natural landscape which may be considered built heritage was the successful application in 1994 by archaeologists in Bedfordshire, England to have a medieval rabbit warren declared a protected ancient monument: Historic England Website [7].

[12] South China Morning Post [12].

the loss of the culture and heritage of the neighbourhood as a community with the consequent psychological effect this has on the people of this neighbourhood.[13]

It should also be noted that, as the term "cultural heritage" may refer to negative or dark heritage, evidence of the activities of humankind which should be remembered because of the terrible things humans have done to each other and the environment. Therefore, the term "built heritage" will also be used to refer to evidence of the negative activities of humans in Hong Kong, for example evidence of the Japanese occupation of Hong Kong, including buildings and areas where atrocities were committed.[14]

1.2 What Built Heritage in Hong Kong?

Hong Kong is a modern vibrant city and famous for its glass and steel skyscrapers. Thus, many would not consider Hong Kong to have much in the way of built heritage. However, Hong Kong has a surprisingly rich built heritage. There are examples of built heritage which predate the colonial occupation in 1841.[15] This is true even on Hong Kong Island, which is often claimed to have been virtually uninhabited before the colonial period. For example, the rock carving, discovered in 2018, at Cape Collinson, Chai Wan, which may date to the Bronze Age,[16] and the Hung Shing Temple, Ap Lei Chau, built by the local community in the 38th year of the reign of Qianlong (1773) for the worship of Hung Shing.[17] Similarly, there are examples of pre-colonial built heritage in Kowloon. For example, the Hau Wong Temple, Kowloon City, which was probably built in 1730.[18] Kowloon also has Hong Kong's oldest preserved archaeological site open to the public, the Lei Cheng UK Han Tomb Museum in Sham Shui Po. This is a 2000-year-old four-chambered Eastern Han dynasty tomb believed to have been built between 25 and 225 A.D.[19] The site was discovered in 1955 and has been preserved with a gallery built alongside to display the artefacts discovered inside. Its discovery was instrumental in the development of Hong Kong's first and only statute intended to protect its heritage, the Antiquities and Monuments Ordinance (cap. 53). Thus there are a large number of

---

[13] South China Morning Post et al. [16].

[14] For example, the punishment ground next to the Japanese headquarters in Sai Kung which is now a kindergarten.

[15] Hong Kong was ceded to Great Britain in perpetuity at the end of the First Opium War (1839–1842), initially in the Convention of Chuenpi, 1841, and then confirmed in the Treaty of Nanking in 1842.

[16] Declared a monument in 2019. AMO 121.

[17] Declared a monument in 2014. AMO 107.

[18] Declared a monument in 2014. AMO 108.

[19] Leisure and Cultural Services Website. Lei Cheng UK Han Tomb Museum [8].

archaeological sites, Chinese temples, colonial churches and other religious, military and government buildings of heritage significance on Hong Kong Island and in Kowloon.

There are many more historical buildings in the New Territories and the Islands which form part of the New Territories. The New Territories was incorporated into Hong Kong in 1898 with an already well-recognised indigenous population with many fortified villages, temples and cultivated areas.[20] For example, the Yeung Hau Temple, Tai O, which was probably built in 1699 or earlier as evidenced by the oldest relic at the temple, an iron bell cast in the 38th year of Kangxi reign (1699) of the Qing dynasty.[21] There are also examples of built heritage constructed after 1841 but before the British leasing of the New Territories, as the indigenous population benefited economically from their proximity to Hong Kong and new residents joined them in what was to become the New Territories in 1898. For example, Hung Shing Temple, Kau Sai Chau (Island), Sai Kung. According to local history and the stone tablet at the temple, the building was built before 1889.[22] This economic benefit is also seen in the renovation of earlier built heritage. For example, the Kang Yung Study Hall, in Sheung Wo Hang, Sha Tau Kok, was renovated by the Li clan in 1872.[23] The Chinese authorities also built buildings in this period to deal with the problems the British colony caused and to benefit from its trade, even if it was a trade that had been frowned upon. For example, the Viceroy of Guangdong and Guangxi ordered the establishment of three customs stations in 1868 at Fat Tau Chau, Cheung Chau and Kap Shui Mun (Ma Wan) respectively to collect *likin* (tax) on opium trade. These stations ceased to operate in 1899 after the lease of the New Territories to Britain. The site of the Fat Tau Chau Old Chinese Customs Station was discovered in 1962 and declared a monument in 1983.[24]

1.3 Problems for Built Heritage in Hong Kong

The built heritage of Hong Kong has faced and is facing many problems in common with built heritage around the world. Of course, in addition, built heritage in Hong Kong has also faced and is facing its own particular problems.

---

[20] The New Territories were leased to the British by the Qing in 1898 in the Second Convention of Peking for a term of 99 years.

[21] Declared a monument in 2017. AMO 117.

[22] Declared a monument in 2002. AMO 76.

[23] Declared a monument in 1991. AMO 44.

[24] AMO 18.

1.3.1 Common Problems for Built Heritage in Hong Kong

Hong Kong faces the same problems as other cities considering heritage preservation. Possibly the most commonly ignored but most significant factor affecting the conservation of built heritage is time. All built heritage deteriorates and needs maintenance: as soon as a building is completed it must be maintained—and this is expensive. Many old buildings require intensive maintenance using crafts, skills and materials which may no longer be easily available, and which are time consuming, difficult and, consequently, expensive. Often it is easier and cheaper to demolish an old building and replace it with a new structure which is made from cheaper materials, using fast building techniques and which is compliant with new building safety standards and requirements, and more energy efficient.

As with other jurisdictions, Hong Kong's built heritage may also be under threat from environmental issues such as pollution, weather and climate change.[25] Pollution is a threat to built heritage in Hong Kong, as, along with most other high population density areas, its built heritage may be damaged by pollutants such as acid rain which literally eat away at the fabric of its buildings.[26] Hong Kong's extremes of temperatures and heavy rainfall may damage the fabric of buildings, with wood rotting and stone cracking. Recently climate change and consequent rising sea levels have become a concern in Hong Kong because of the high proportion of reclaimed land and the fact that most developed land is coastal and low lying. There have been concerns that Tai O, the fishing village built on stilts above the water of the coast of the island of Lantau, sometimes referred to as "the Venice of Hong Kong", might become submerged by rising sea water so that its residents might have to leave.[27] The village is often flooded during typhoons but this problem may become worse with rising sea levels and climate change.

Perhaps the most important examples of the natural and man-made threats from the environment to heritage in Hong Kong are those affecting Victoria Harbour. The Victoria Harbour is encroached on both sides by land reclamation and development. Nature deposits silts in its waters and man deposits his waste. As a busy and important part of Hong Kong, it needs constant expensive repair of sea walls, dredging and clearing of channels to make sure it is navigable and safeguarded. Climate change affects its waters in consistency, living organisms, pollutants distributed by changing ocean flows and, at a fundamental level—the level of its waters.

---

[25] For example, in Venice, apart from concerns over the rising sea level and sinking city, there have been concerns that pigeons have damaged historic buildings. In Florence concern has been expressed regarding its palaces and churches because of damage by "time, pollution, lack of funds and regular maintenance".

[26] This is a problem in other jurisdictions. For example, in India the Taj Mahal is believed to be under threat from pollution and its human visitors. The Guardian. Jason Burke [20]; Time Magazine [21].

[27] South China Morning Post and Ng [14].

1.3.2 Particular Problems for Built Heritage in Hong Kong

Hong Kong has been inhabited since the Neolithic period and archaeologists have discovered artefacts dating back 6000 years.[28] However, first impressions for many visitors to Hong Kong are that there are not many examples of built heritage readily visible which evidence this rich past—this is particularly the case on Hong Kong Island. Even buildings of the colonial period have been subject to multiple replacements because of the ever increasing demands for space for business and living. This demand is exacerbated by the lack of developable space in Hong Kong because of its topography.

Although the Hong Kong Special Administrative Region covers some 1104 km^2 made up of Hong Kong Island, the Kowloon Peninsula, the New Territories and 262 outlying islands, less than 25% of this space has been developed and most that remains undeveloped provides challenges to development because of slopes and soil conditions.[29] In fact Hong Kong has a very high proportion of reclaimed land with many coastal developments being based upon massive reclamations.

In addition, Hong Kong has faced a rapid increase in population in the last 70 years. Hong Kong's overcrowding problems have been exacerbated because of economic and political immigration from Mainland China. The population of Hong Kong increased threefold from 2.2 million in 1950 to 6.7 million in 2001,[30] with two important factors being those fleeing the People's Republic of China after the Revolution of 1949 and those seeking economic opportunity after the return of Hong Kong to the People's Republic of China in 1997.[31] In the By-census of 2016 the official population was recorded as over 7.3 million.[32]

Therefore, with such a large population and such a small area of developable land, Hong Kong is one of the most densely populated areas in the world.[33] Thus, a consistent problem facing built heritage protection in Hong Kong has been the simple law of supply and demand: as the demand for land has exceeded supply the price of land has increased to such an extent that new developments are encouraged to be of higher rise buildings to maximise return from the land. This constant pressure to replace old buildings with higher and bigger developments has resulted in the modern Hong Kong skyline and the loss of many old buildings: for example, David Lung has noted that Norman Foster's distinctive headquarters building for the Hong

---

[28] *Soaring Phoenix Rising Dragon*, Celebratory Exhibition for the 50th Anniversary of the Chinese University of Hong Kong.

[29] GovHK. Hong Kong—the Facts [5].

[30] Government Statistics Office. Hong Kong's Population: Characteristics and Trends [4].

[31] Hong Kong's official population statistics recorded 7,241,700 in mid-2014. GovHK. Hong Kong the Facts [6].

[32] The Government of the Hong Kong Special Administrative Region of the People's Republic of China. Hong Kong By-census 2016 Results [17].

[33] The Government of the Hong Kong Special Administrative Region of the People's Republic of China. Hong Kong Census [18].

Kong and Shanghai Bank in Central is the fourth building to occupy that position in 150 years.[34]

The Second World War is also an important reason that there are few examples of built heritage remaining on Hong Kong Island or in Kowloon. With the focus on the destruction of heritage in Europe it is often forgotten or deliberately overlooked that Asia suffered terrible devastation to its people and heritage. Hong Kong was subject to intensive aerial bombardment by Japanese and American forces, the legacy of which is still with us today in the form of the regular discovery of unexploded ordinance.[35]

The destruction of built heritage in the New Territories has been less driven by development, as it has only recently seen a similar demand for land for building as in the older urban areas of Hong Kong Island and Kowloon. This is because it was considered difficult to travel to and road and rail connections have only relatively recently been improved to permit easy commuting from the New Territories into the commercial areas.

Perhaps a unique problem which has faced Hong Kong's built heritage is the identification of Hong Kong as a temporary or borrowed place. The idea of Hong Kong as a temporary place has many contributing causes. For many of its residents since its founding and continuing today, Hong Kong has been considered a temporary or transient place. In colonial times many expatriates came to Hong Kong intending to make money and leave. Many of the Chinese who came to Hong Kong were fleeing the mainland, perhaps because of the oppression of the Qing, the chaos of civil war, Japanese invasion, communist revolution, consequent austerity, famine, and/or simply as economic migrants. These residents often did not see Hong Kong as a permanent place of residence but a temporary refuge on a flight to family and/or opportunity in other jurisdictions or in the hope that they might one day be able to return to their homes in the mainland. One former Governor of Hong Kong, Alexander Grantham,[36] described Hong Kong as a "Railway Station".[37] Thus there was little concern shown by the people or government of colonial Hong Kong to protect or preserve buildings or landscapes.

In addition, the British colonial government's original decision to use leasehold as the land tenure system in the colony with duration of the lease terms varying depending on the location within Hong Kong also reinforced the idea that no structure or building was or is permanent. The idea that Hong Kong is a temporary place was also reinforced by the British acquisition of the New Territories, the largest land area of the Hong Kong SAR, by way of lease from the Chinese.[38] This was in contrast to the acquisition of Hong Kong Island in perpetuity and Kowloon by *faux* lease

---

[34] Lung [9].

[35] South China Morning Post et al. [13].

[36] Governor of Hong Kong 1947–57.

[37] Grantham (1965) Via Ports. Hong Kong University Press, Hong Kong.

[38] The Convention between the United Kingdom and China, Respecting an Extension of Hong Kong Territory, commonly known as the Second Convention of Peking, 9 June 1898.

1.3 Problems for Built Heritage in Hong Kong

and then in perpetuity as the spoils of war.[39] This leasing of the largest land area of Hong Kong with its intrinsic sense of an end date to colonial occupation has also been identified as giving Hong Kong the identity of a "Borrowed Place."[40] Thus, in the New Territories, leased by the British in 1898 for a term of 99 years, leases of land from the colonial government had to be restricted to less than the British lease term and therefore were originally granted for 50 years and then extended to 98 years. With the return of the New Territories to the People's Republic of China along with the rest of Hong Kong in 1997, leases were extended to 2047.[41] This is the date agreed between China and Britain for the continuation of Hong Kong's government and legal system under China's "One Country-Two Systems" policy,[42] given effect in Hong Kong's mini-constitution, the Basic Law.[43] On Hong Kong Island and in Kowloon longer leases were originally granted. However, the future of these land holdings is also in doubt after 2047, Many see this important date with little clarification of political system or property ownership after this date as another illustration of Hong Kong's temporary status.

Another factor that may be particular to Hong Kong was the concern the colonial government had for any of its decisions upsetting its powerful neighbour. Thus, Elizabeth Sinn noted in 1987 that, "It is said that in 1957, when the Antiquities laws were first being drafted, Hong Kong authorities approached the Chinese government to sound out their opinion on the preservation of "'Chinese' archaeological finds."[44] This is interesting as the concept of heritage at an international and domestic level is often political, and the identification of heritage, particularly at international and often at domestic levels, is usually political. But for Hong Kong under the British government and perhaps even more today, all administrative decisions are made with the object of causing as little disturbance in Beijing as possible. Sinn noted that colonial governments did not have the national focus that a national government would have on emphasising history and heritage, thus the British colonial government did not have an impetus to conserve. Sinn also noted the "infamous circumstances" in which the British acquired the colony of Hong Kong impacted on the colonial government's attitude to the history and heritage of the colony. Thus, they may have

---

[39] Harry Smith Parkes, Esquire, one of the Allied Commissioners for the Government of the City of Canton, first leased the territory of the southern part of Kowloon from the Chinese on 20 March 1860, on behalf of Great Britain. However, on 18 October 1860 the Convention of Peking (usually referred to as the "First Convention of Peking") was signed and ceded Kowloon, south of Boundary Street, to the British.

[40] See for example, Welsh [23].

[41] New Territories Leases (Extension) Ordinance (cap. 150). 26 February 1988.

[42] Joint Declaration of the Government of the United Kingdom of Great Britain and Northern Ireland and the Government of the People's Republic of China on the Question of Hong Kong, 19 December 1984 (Sino-British Joint Declaration).

[43] The Government of the Hong Kong Special Administrative Region of the People's Republic of China. The Basic Law of the Hong Kong Special Administrative Region of the People's Republic of China [19].

[44] Sinn [11], at p. 166.

been inclined to "let sleeping dogs lie".[45] Arguably, this attitude was inherited and promoted by the post-colonial governments.

At this point it should be noted that Hong Kong has received particular criticism because in many other cities in China the preservation of built heritage is seen as an important social and economic factor in urban planning. For example, Xi'an and Guangzhou have expended much and foregone lucrative development in their preservation of many aspects of their built heritage, so why not in Hong Kong? There has been suspicion that the preservation of evidence of Hong Kong's colonial past is embarrassing and that is why there is no priority to protect buildings associated with its colonial past. However, in cities such as Shanghai and Guangzhou evidence of the colonial past is protected and celebrated, even if this is for a very particular political narrative.[46]

A further issue in the debate about built heritage, and instrumental in its successful preservation in Hong Kong, has been the focus of social and political unrest on attempts by the post-colonial government to remove built heritage linked to Hong Kong's colonial past. Thus, the preservation of Hong Kong's built heritage is now more of a social and political issue than it ever was under British rule. Post-colonial Hong Kong has seen far more public criticism of and demonstration, sometimes violent, against the redevelopment of built heritage than was ever seen under the colonial government. For example, the movement of the Queen's Pier, and the proposed development of public sites, such as the Police Married Quarters in Hollywood Road.[47] There has also been public outcry over the loss of built heritage on privately owned sites, for example Ho Tung Gardens on the Peak. The issues involving these elements of Hong Kong's built heritage have highlighted the inadequacy of the legal and regulatory framework that is intended to protect the built heritage and, even more than this, and perhaps more distressing, the lack of government will to use even these outdated and inadequate measures to protect Hong Kong's built heritage.

Therefore, when built heritage is identified in Hong Kong the people of Hong Kong face a similar dilemma to those in other urban centres, the dilemma of balancing needs for commercial and domestic space against attempts to retain built heritage. However, in Hong Kong the decision about developing built heritage sites is not just a straight choice between developing and preserving, with the consequent issues of loss of heritage or loss of commercial and public utility, and conflict between private property rights as opposed to public concern for heritage. The question is further exacerbated by all the additional pressures and complicating factors specific to Hong Kong noted above. Of course, it may be argued that the peculiar nature and circumstances of Hong Kong have meant this has not been much of a dilemma

---

[45] Sinn [11], at p. 163.

[46] See, for example, the preservation of colonial building on Shamian Island in Guangzhou in spite, or perhaps because of, the Islands' and the buildings' associations with the Opium Wars. See Wikipedia. Shamian [24].

[47] PMQ, "Police Married Quarters" Website [10].

1.3 Problems for Built Heritage in Hong Kong

Fig. 1.1 Murray House, formerly in Central now in Stanley

in Hong Kong until recent years, as Hong Kong's successive governments have not considered heritage preservation rather focussing on overcrowding, sanitation, development, economic gain and political survival- all legitimate concerns. However, a framework for protection of built heritage was developed in Hong Kong, and this development is considered in the next chapter (Figs. 1.1 and 1.2).

Fig. 1.2 Sung Wong Toi as it is today

References

1. Antiquities Advisory Board (2014) Respecting our heritage while looking ahead: policy on conservation of built heritage consultation paper. https://www.gov.hk/en/residents/government/publication/consultation/docs/2014/CBH.pdf Accessed 10 June 2021

References

2. Antiquities and Monuments Office website. Declared Monuments in Hong Kong. http://www.amo.gov.hk/en/monuments_nt.php. Accessed 8 June 2021
3. Gallagher SB (2020) Prošek or Prosecco: intellectual property or intangible cultural heritage? In: Chaisse J, Dias Simões F, Friedmann D (eds) Wine law and policy: from national terroirs to a global market. Brill Nijhoff, Leiden
4. Government Statistics Office. Hong Kong's population: characteristics and trends. http://www.info.gov.hk/info/population/eng/pdf/chapter2_e.pdf. Accessed 8 June 2021
5. GovHK. Hong Kong—the Facts. http://www.gov.hk/en/about/abouthk/facts.htm. Accessed 8 June 2021
6. GovHK. Hong Kong the Facts. http://www.gov.hk/en/about/abouthk/factsheets/docs/population.pdf. Accessed 8 June 2021
7. Historic England Website (1994) Listing List, 25 November 1994. A medieval warren on Dunstable Downs: https://historicengland.org.uk/listing/the-list/list-entry/1009398. Accessed 8 June 2021
8. Leisure and Cultural Services Website. Lei Cheng Uk Han Tomb Museum. http://www.lcsd.gov.hk/CE/Museum/History/en_US/web/mh/about-us/lei-cheng-uk-han-tomb-museum.html. Accessed 8 June 2021
9. Lung D (2012) Built heritage in transition: a critique of Hong Kong's conservation movement and the antiquities and monuments ordinance. Hong Kong Law J 42(1):121–141
10. PMQ, Police Married Quarters Website. http://www.pmq.org.hk/heritage/history-of-pmq/. Accessed 8 June 2021
11. Sinn E (1987) Modernization without tears: attempts at cultural heritage conservation in Hong Kong. Paper presented at the symposium on cultural heritage and modernization held in Hong Kong, 29 September to 2 October 1987. Reprinted in full in Meacham W (2015) The struggle for Hong Kong's heritage—narrative, documents and reminiscences of the early years. Published by the Author, Hong Kong. Chapter 9, at p.166
12. South China Morning Post (2013) Is Pok Fu Lam worth naming as heritage site?" http://www.scmp.com/comment/insight-opinion/article/1335394/pok-fu-lam-worth-naming-heritage-site. Accessed 8 June 2021
13. South China Morning Post, Leung C, Ng N, Yeung R (2018) Major evacuation continues after second bomb found at Hong Kong site where 450 kg wartime explosive unearthed at weekend. http://www.scmp.com/print/news/hong-kong/law-crime/article/2131341/second-bomb-found-hong-kong-site-where-450kg-wartime. Accessed 8 June 2021
14. South China Morning Post, Ng Y (2018) Could rising tides put the Venice of Hong Kong underwater? https://www.scmp.com/news/hong-kong/health-environment/article/2136451/could-rising-tides-put-hong-kongs-tai-o-underwater. Accessed 8 June 2021
15. South China Morning Post, Peters E (2021) Colonial-era Murray House's resurrection in Hong Kong 20 years on: heritage expert still sceptical, Stanley villagers happy it draws visitors. https://www.scmp.com/lifestyle/travel-leisure/article/3119722/colonial-era-murray-houses-resurrection-hong-kong-20-years. Accessed 11 June 2021
16. South China Morning Post. Solum A, Ka-sing A (2017) Sham Shui Po cultural heritage under threat as neighbourhood modernises. https://www.scmp.com/video/hong-kong/2107987/sham-shui-po-cultural-heritage-under-threat-neighbourhood-modernises. Accessed 8 June 2021
17. The Government of the Hong Kong Special Administrative Region of the People's Republic of China. Hong Kong By-census 2016 Results: https://www.bycensus2016.gov.hk/en/bc-mt.html. Accessed 8 June 2021
18. The Government of the Hong Kong Special Administrative Region of the People's Republic of China. Hong Kong Census 2011: http://www.census2011.gov.hk/pdf/summary-results.pdf. Accessed 8 June 2021
19. The Government of the Hong Kong Special Administrative Region of the People's Republic of China. The Basic Law of the Hong Kong Special Administrative Region of the People's Republic of China. https://www.basiclaw.gov.hk/en/basiclaw/index.html. Accessed 8 June 2021.

20. The Guardian, Burke J (2010) Taj Mahal threatened by polluted air and water. https://www.theguardian.com/world/2010/dec/02/taj-mahal-threatened-pollution. Accessed 8 June 2021
21. Time Magazine (2018) The Taj Mahal Is changing color. That has India's Highest Court Concerned. http://time.com/5262395/taj-mahal-india-change-color-supreme-court/ Accessed 8 June 2021
22. UNESCO (2019) Second Consultation on the 2011 recommendation on historic urban landscape: implementation by member states. http://whc.unesco.org/en/activities/638/. Accessed 8 June 2021
23. Welsh F (1993) A Borrowed place: the history of Hong Kong. Kodansha International, New York
24. Wikipedia, Shamian. https://en.wikipedia.org/wiki/Shamian. Accessed 8 June 2021

Chapter 2
The Development of Protection for Built Heritage in Hong Kong up to 1976

Abstract Built heritage protection in Hong Kong has followed the progression common to most cities. These common factors of building and preserving monuments to wealth and power result in the preservation of certain buildings and sites in most cities, as is the case in Hong Kong. At the end of the nineteenth century and the beginning of the twentieth century Hong Kong introduced statutory protection for individual sites, for example Sung Wong Toi and the Man Mo Temple in Hollywood Road. Hong Kong also introduced general ordinances that indirectly provided protection for Hong Kong's built heritage. The Second World War had a drastic impact on Hong Kong's built heritage, with significant losses. In the rebuilding of Hong Kong after the War, and the need to house the influx of people, the discovery of the Han tomb at Lei Cheng UK, Sham Shui Po, in 1955, led to the drafting of the Antiquities and Monuments Bill and its gazetting as Ordinance in 1971.

2.1 Introduction

It is only relatively recently that general laws have been adopted in most jurisdictions to protect built heritage. Before the advent of general laws to protect built heritage the preservation and/or conservation of built heritage in most jurisdictions occurred on an ad hoc basis. This only involved the law as general property protection laws—for example private law rights against damage to property, and public laws such as those restricting development and criminalising damage to property. Therefore, ad hoc protection of built heritage often began with wealthy and powerful individuals, groups or the state protecting built heritage important to them as a symbol of their wealth and power. Many examples of built heritage have been preserved because their owners appreciated them and provided the necessary care and funds for their maintenance and survival. Apart from the love and care of the owners of built heritage, it has usually been conserved and/or preserved because of its importance to a powerful group in society or the state itself. Thus, the common examples of built heritage which have been preserved in societies around the world are those linked to power and religion—either of which may result in protection of built heritage and both of which often have played a part in such protection, as power and religion have been and are interrelated in most societies. Thus, many fortified buildings, for example castles in Europe and Asia, have been preserved because they represented the power of the state and were symbols of authority. In China we can see the palaces of the emperors, the fortified walls around cities such as Xi'an, and the Great Wall as examples of buildings which are symbols of power and/or fortifications. Similarly, in China many temples and other religious buildings have been preserved because they were valued as symbols of the power of the religions they represented and linked to the power of the ruling elite, for example the Temple of Heaven in Beijing was protected as a religious, social and political symbol.

If not protected by its owners, or the rich and powerful and, again, these were usually the same, most built heritage was subject to removal and development of its site as society needed. Built heritage may even have been destroyed for the robbing of its raw materials for other building projects.

However, there are also examples of built heritage which have survived without conscious protection. These have usually survived because their site was of little value to contemporary needs. The site may also have been too awkward to get to or too far from contemporary building projects to make it viable to rob the materials it was constructed of. Further, sometimes sites and buildings were not considered important or just forgotten, or, if not forgotten, were avoided because of superstition—thus the failure of memory and ghosts have played a role in the survival of some of the world's most important built heritage.[1]

Today, most jurisdictions have specific laws which are intended to provide some protection for built heritage. We will now consider how this protection developed in Hong Kong.

2.2 The Development of Protection for Built Heritage in Hong Kong

When societies have consciously developed protection for their built heritage they have often followed a relatively common pattern. This was identified by Carol Rose in her seminal article as involving three dominant perspectives in the development of historic preservation[2]:

1. Seeking to inspire the observer with a sense of patriotism;
2. Cultural, artistic and architectural focus: "preservation activities should focus on the artistic merit of buildings and on the integrity of their architectural style."
3. The combination of the first two perspectives with a "concern for the environmental and psychological effects of historic preservation."

---

[1] For example, although the Pyramids of Giza and the Great Wall of China have all been subject to robbing for materials at times, they have also been avoided for superstitious reasons, and, particularly for parts of the Great Wall, because it is difficult to remove materials from them.

[2] Rose [21], 473.

2.2 The Development of Protection for Built Heritage in Hong Kong

Although Rose developed her perspectives considering protection in the United States of America, we can see parallels in many jurisdictions if we substitute terms. In particular, if we look for other common objectives instead of patriotism. Thus, in colonial Hong Kong, a borrowed place, where inhabitants expected to only stay for a relatively short period, we may replace the concept of patriotism with the worship of wealth and power. Therefore, the development of heritage preservation in Hong Kong followed three dominant perspectives which now often overlap:

1. Seeking to inspire the observer with awe for wealth and power;
2. Cultural, artistic and historical focus;
3. The combination of the first two perspectives with a "concern for the environmental and psychological effects of" heritage preservation.

These perspectives apply for both private and public protection of built heritage.

Thus, private persons, both living and non-living (in the form of corporations), have often built and protected examples of built heritage to show their wealth and power. We may consider the great and imposing buildings of the banks and other financial institutions, for example the Old Bank of China Building in Central. Of course, Hong Kong's particular circumstances have also meant the banks have often replaced their old buildings with modern buildings to show their wealth and power as well. Perhaps a better example has been the endowing of public buildings by wealthy and powerful individuals, for example, Sir Hormusjee N. Mody's donation to pay for the main building of the University of Hong Kong.[3] In addition, the wealthy and powerful have often preserved built heritage to show their wealth and power, for example the powerful families of the New Territories have preserved their ancestral halls, religious buildings and other examples of built heritage including graves. In addition to emphasising their wealth and power, this protection has also emphasised the second perspective, a cultural and historical focus, as it has emphasised their links to Hong Kong's past. This has undoubtedly served a political and economic purpose as well.

Similarly, with public protection for built heritage we see the initial focus on the example of wealth and power, moving to the cultural and historical and finally these perspectives are joined by a recognition of the public concern for the environmental and psychological effects of preserving built heritage. This third perspective of heritage preservation is also now apparent among private persons in their individual effort to protect the built heritage they own, and also in the social movements that have campaigned for built heritage protection in Hong Kong.

In noting these perspectives in the public protection of built heritage in Hong Kong we may divide the development of built heritage protection in Hong Kong into four temporal phases:

1. The beginnings of built heritage protection in Hong Kong up to 1976;
2. The implementation of the Antiquities and Monuments Ordinance in 1976;
3. The effects of the Antiquities and Monuments Ordinance on built heritage pre-1997;

---

[3] South China Morning Post [25].

4. The Hong Kong (SAR) and built heritage post-1997.

The significant dates being the implementation of the Antiquities and Monuments Ordinance in 1976 and the end of Hong Kong as a British colony in 1997 and its return to China.

2.3 The Beginnings of Built Heritage Protection in Hong Kong

In Hong Kong our first records of built heritage protection pre-date the British colony and are usually inscriptions in temples detailing repair and renovation and listing those who paid for this. In the Colony of Hong Kong, built heritage protection began for examples of built heritage which emphasised that Hong Kong was a permanent part of the British Empire which was wealthy, powerful and enduring. Thus, the first example of what may be considered built heritage protection was the building and opening of St. John's Cathedral in 1849. The Cathedral was built in the traditional English gothic style popular in England at the time. The protection of this building and the intention for it to remain a permanent structure in Hong was signalled by the fact that it is Hong Kong's only freehold land granted by the colonial government.[4]

Apart from the Cathedral, the British then built structures to symbolise the wealth and power of the British Empire. For example, Government House, originally the British colonial governor's house built in 1855 in a prominent position above the city of Victoria and Victoria Harbour.[5] This was maintained in its original style with notable remodelling by the Japanese during the wartime occupation (1941–1945). Similarly, although a later structure, the Supreme Court Building in Central, built in 1912, also epitomizes the power of British colonial rule with its Royal Arms carved in stone above its entrance—part of the exterior protected as a gazetted monument, possibly to the embarrassment of some in Hong Kong today.[6]

Apart from buildings linked to colonial power other buildings which received protection were linked to other manifestations of power, for example churches and temples, or they may just have been protected by the state or powerful factions within the state because of the ideas they represented and/or support and/or legitimacy they gave these factions.

---

[4] Church of England Trust Ordinance (Cap.1014), Section 6(1).
[5] AMO 59.
[6] AMO 26.

2.3.1 First Statutory Protection of Built Heritage in Hong Kong- Special Ordinances

As in many jurisdictions Hong Kong's protection of its built heritage by legislation began with piecemeal identification of specific examples which were deemed worthy of protection by specific laws. There would also be general ordinances which affected built heritage. In Hong Kong, as examples of the former, there is the legislation to protect Sung Wong Toi and the Man Mo Temple in Hollywood Road. As examples of the latter there is the Lands Resumption Ordinance, the Chinese Temples Ordinance, the Buildings Ordinance etc. These are considered individually.

2.3.1.1 Sung Wong Toi Reservation Ordinance, 1899

Hong Kong's first law to protect built heritage was the decision by the Legislative Council in 1899 to preserve the site of Sung Wong Toi rock and the "Sacred Hill" near Kowloon City.[7] This was a large boulder with an inscription to commemorate the last two boy emperors of the Southern Song dynasty, Zhao Shi and Zhao Bing, who were in Hong Kong from 1277 to 1279 escaping their enemies. Unfortunately, when fleeing their enemies after they left Hong Kong, one died of natural causes and the other committed suicide to avoid capture with the help of a loyal follower. The Legislators' debate about protecting the site references a specification at the time the 1860. Treaty was made between Britain and China for the original leasing of Kowloon that the rock inscription and hill should be protected. Thus heritage protection may have begun under the influence of international negotiation in Hong Kong.

The Legislative Council passed the Sung Wong Toi Reservation Ordinance in 1899.[8] In this Ordinance the piece of Crown land in Kowloon known as "Sung Wong Toi or Sung Wong Tong":

> shall not be let for building or other purposes, but shall be reserved as a place of popular resort. and of antiquarian interest: Provided, nevertheless, that if at any time hereafter it appears to the Governor that it is necessary, in the interests either of the Imperial Government or of the Government of this Colony, that such land should be re-appropriated, either wholly or in part. it shall be lawful for the Governor to re-appropriate such land of any part thereof, and to use it or allow it to be used for other purposes than those above mentioned.[9]

The governor in council could make regulations for "the maintenance of good order in the said reserved land, and for the preservation, management, and use thereof, and for the enjoyment thereof by the public".[10] Any breach of these regulations could be penalised by a penalty on summary conviction of a maximum of twenty-five dollars.

---

[7] See Meacham [15], at pp. 4–11.
[8] Historical Laws of Hong Kong Online [9].
[9] Historical Laws of Hong Kong Onlines [10], Sections 1 and 2.
[10] Sung Wong Toi Reservation Ordinance, Section 3.

The Ordinance then provided that,[11] "Every person who injures or defaces any ancient monument, rock, memorial, or inscription which is on or upon any land reserved under this Ordinance shall upon summary conviction be liable either to a fine not exceeding fifty dollars, and, in addition thereto, to pay such sum as the magistrate may think just for the purpose of repairing any damage which has been caused, or to imprisonment for any term not exceeding one month".

Despite the legislators' commitment to protect the site it was nearly sold in 1915 by the Hong Kong Government Department of Works for redevelopment. Luckily locals discovered the plan and objected to the governor who agreed it would not be sold. Private donations were then used to construct gardens and walkways around the hill. Unfortunately, the rock and hill were levelled by the Japanese in 1943 to extend the airport during the war. Part of the rock was discovered after the war and now stands in Ma Tau Chung in Kowloon.[12]

2.3.1.2 Man Mo Temple Ordinance, 1908

The Man Mo Temple Compound Hollywood Road, Sheung Wan was built between 1847 and 1862 by wealthy Chinese merchants. It was officially entrusted to Tung Wah Hospital with the enactment of the Man Mo Temple Ordinance in 1908. The Ordinance noted that most of the founders were now dead and that the Directors of the Tung Wah Hospital had been effectively managing the "hereditaments and premises and the temple". Therefore, the Ordinance vested "all the messuages, lands, tenements and hereditaments…and all other properties and moneys now belonging to or in the possession or under the control of the Man Mo Temple…in the Tung wa [sic] hospital".[13] Therefore, the Tung Wah Hospital group had effective control over the Temple and its lands, holding it under a trust as the Man Mo Temple Fund.[14] However, the Hospital could not sell or mortgage the land without the approval and signature of the governor.[15] The fund was to be used for the upkeep of the Temple and its religious purposes, with special provisions for the Directors of the Hospital to use surplus finds for charitable purposes.[16] The Temple was declared a monument in 2010.[17]

---

[11] Sung Wong Toi Reservation Ordinance, Section 4.

[12] See the comments of Mr Cheung Yan-Lung in the Official Report of Proceedings of the Hong Kong Legislative Council, 16th June 1982 [18].

[13] Historical Laws of Hong Kong Online [10].

[14] Man Mo Temple Ordinance, 1908, Section 7.

[15] Man Mo Temple Ordinance, 1908, Section 4.

[16] Man Mo Temple Ordinance, 1908, Section 8.

[17] AMO 96.

2.3.2 First Statutory Protection of Built Heritage in Hong Kong—General Ordinances

There are a number of general ordinances that may affect built heritage because of restrictions on what may be done with land or buildings, or because they provide for the care of particular types of buildings. For example: the Lands Resumption Ordinance (Cap.124); the Chinese Temples Ordinance (Cap.153); the Church of England Trust Ordinance (Cap.1014); the Town Planning Ordinance (Cap.131); the Buildings Ordinance (Cap. 123); the Antiquities and Monuments Ordinance (Cap 53); the Urban Renewal Authority Ordinance (Cap. 563), Country Parks Ordinance (Cap. 208); the Mass Transit Railway (Land Resumption and Related Provisions) Ordinance (Cap. 276); the Demolished Buildings (Re-Development of Sites) Ordinance (Cap. 337); the Environment and Conservation Fund Ordinance (Cap. 450); and the Environmental Impact Assessment Ordinance (Cap. 499).

The Church of England Trust Ordinance (Cap.1014), 1930, provides for the incorporation of a body of trustees to hold property for the purposes of the Church of England, and to provide for the performance of divine worship according to the rites and ceremonies of the Church of England. An important aspect of this for Hong Kong's built heritage is that it provides that St John's Cathedral is vested in these trustees and conforms this is as "fee simple".[18] Thus, it is the only land in Hong Kong not provided by the Hong Kong SAR on a lease or licence. The Cathedral was one of the last monuments declared by the colonial government in 1996.[19]

The most important general legislation which may affect built heritage was implemented as outlined in the Table 2.1.

We can deal briefly with each of these ordinances, but will deal in more detail with the Antiquities and Monuments Ordinance, the Environmental Impact Assessment Ordinance and the Urban Renewal Authority Ordinance as we follow the story of the development of legal protection for built heritage in Hong Kong.

The Lands Resumption Ordinance (Cap.124), 1911, mandated the government to take back land for public purposes Therefore, it could have been used to facilitate the resuming of land by the government because it contained built heritage—there is no record of this ever being a consideration.

Of course in the development of Hong Kong's legal protection for built heritage we see other fortuitous events such as scandals in the administration of Chinese Temples which led to legislation to deal with misappropriation of funds—the Chinese Temples Ordinance of 1928. In seeking to prevent further misappropriations the colonial government's legislation included provisions which have been used to protect and maintain Chinese Temples in Hong Kong.[20] The Ordinance set up the Chinese Temples Committee to oversee the finances and administration of designated Chinese

---

[18] Church of England Trust Ordinance, Section 6.
[19] AMO 60.
[20] Home Affairs Bureau [12].

Table 2.1 Legislation which may affect built heritage in Hong Kong

Title and date	Purpose
Lands Resumption Ordinance (Cap.124), 1911	To facilitate the resumption of Government lands required for public purposes
Chinese Temples Ordinance (Cap.153), 1928	To register and provide for the governance of Chinese temples
Town Planning Ordinance (Cap.131), 1939, amended 1991	To promote the health, safety, convenience and general welfare of the community by making provision for the systematic preparation and approval of plans for the lay-out of areas of Hong Kong as well as for the types of building suitable for erection therein and for the preparation and approval of plans for areas within which permission is required for development
Buildings Ordinance (Cap 123), 1956	To provide for the planning, design and construction of buildings and associated works; to make provision for the rendering safe of dangerous buildings and land; to make provision for regular inspections of buildings and the associated repairs to prevent the buildings from becoming unsafe; and to make provision for matters connected therewith
Antiquities and Monuments Ordinance (Cap 53), 1971, implemented 1976	To provide for the preservation of objects of historical, archaeological and palaeontological interest and for matters ancillary thereto or connected therewith
Environmental Impact Assessment Ordinance (Cap 499), 1998	To provide for assessing the impact on the environment of certain projects and proposals, for protecting the environment and for incidental matters. Extended in the Chief Executive's policy Address 2007 to include Heritage Impact Assessments
Urban Renewal Authority Ordinance (Cap 563), 2001	To establish the Urban Renewal Authority as a perpetual body to carry out urban renewal

temples.[21] The requirement for registration of Chinese Temples and details of their operation[22] coupled with a statutory obligation to use all revenues for "due observance of the customary ceremonies and the maintenance of the temple buildings and temple properties",[23] ensured the protection and preservation of many temples. For example, the Hau Wong Temple, Kowloon City, probably built in 1730 or before, and patronised by Qing officials and soldiers from the Kowloon Walled City between 1847 and 1899, was taken over by the Chinese Temples Committee in 1928. The

---

[21] Historical Laws of Hong Kong Online [9].
[22] Chinese Temples Ordinance, Section 5.
[23] Chinese Temples Ordinance, Section 8.

2.3 The Beginnings of Built Heritage Protection in Hong Kong

Temple was declared a monument in 2014.[24] Similarly, the Hung Shing Temple in Ap Lei Chau, built by the local community in the 38th year of the reign of Qianlong (1773), was taken over by the Chinese Temples Committee in 1930. The Temple was declared a monument in 2014.[25]

The Town Planning Ordinance (Cap 131), 1939, is intended to control development in Hong Kong to promote the health, safety, convenience and the general welfare of the community. It is administered by the Planning Department with the Town Planning Board. Although heritage is not expressly referred to in the Ordinance, there is a general discretion, which provides the Board may make provision for protection of the environment.[26] Otherwise the Ordinance would only be engaged if an owner of a building or site wished to develop the site and it was subject to a plan, or the owner wished to change the designated use of the building or site. There is no record that built heritage was a consideration in its use before its revision in 1991.

Buildings Ordinance (Cap 123), 1956, provides for the planning, design and construction of buildings and associated works. It also provides for the rendering safe of dangerous buildings and land. All buildings in Hong Kong, unless a "New Territories Exempted House", also known as a "small house", must comply with the Buildings Ordinance in its construction and maintenance.[27] Thus any conservation, preservation and revitalisation works for privately-owned historic buildings in Hong Kong, that may change the original design and approved uses or entail alteration and additions must comply with the prescribed standards under the current Buildings Ordinance (Cap 123) to ensure the safety of users.[28]

The Small House Policy has been another important factor in the development of the built environment in the New Territories. Introduced as an executive measure in 1972, it permits male indigenous residents of villages in existence in the New Territories before 1898 to make a once in a lifetime application for permission to build one house of restricted size for their own use. The ubiquitous use of a design based on Spanish villas has developed the somewhat surreal village landscape of the New Territories.

Although these laws may all affect built heritage, generally if a building has not been declared subject to statutory protection as a proposed monument or declared monument under the Antiquities and Monuments Ordinance then the owner may do as he likes with it subject to the terms of his lease and within the restrictions of the Town Planning Ordinance, restrictions in the Building Ordinance and subject to the common law, for example the tort of nuisance.

---

[24] AMO 108.

[25] AMO 107.

[26] Town Planning Ordinance, Section 4.

[27] Buildings Department Website [4]; see Buildings Ordinance (Application to the New Territories) Ordinance (Cap. 121).

[28] Antiquities Advisory Board [1].

2.4 The Second World War

We have no true idea of the loss that was suffered to buildings, archaeological sites, or the theft of treasures during the Japanese occupation. The Second World War is a period in Hong Kong's history that is not often considered by all but the most courageous of scholars for many reasons and the issue of the loss of heritage during this period has little scholarly record. The Japanese invaded Hong Kong on 8th December 1941 and the British liberated Hong Kong in August 1945. During those three years and eight months of Japanese occupation there was a great deal of destruction and loss to Hong Kong's built heritage with claims that over one quarter of the houses were destroyed,[29] many by Allied bombing. However, there were also some additions to Hong Kong's built heritage. It is known, as previously mentioned, that the Japanese levelled the archaeologically significant site known as Sacred Hill, continuing the Sung Wong Toi rock, at Kai Ta airport to facilitate easier military use of the airport. The Japanese also looted many of Hong Kong's statues, some for their artistic merit, but most for the valuable materials from which they were made. The statues which stood in Statue Square in Central, and from which it derives its name, were looted by the Japanese. The Square was originally known as "Royal Square", because of the statue of Queen Victoria that was sited there in 1896 to celebrate her birthday and in anticipation of her Diamond Jubilee in 1897. This statue was joined by other statues of British Royalty and local eminent figures and so the Square became known as "Statue Square" in English, although it retains the Cantonese name which translates to "Empress' Statue Square." The Japanese removed the statues from Statue Square to send back to Japan. The only one remaining was the Cenotaph, a replica of the one in Whitehall, London, which still stands on the South part of the Square.

The statues removed were[30]:

- Statue of Queen Victoria;
- Statue of Prince Albert, her husband;
- Statue of the Duke of Connaught;
- Statue of Sir Thomas Jackson, 1st Baronet;
- Statue of Edward VII;
- Statue of the Prince of Wales who later became King George V;
- Statue of Queen Alexandra;
- Statue of Mary of Teck, Princess of Wales and future Queen Mary.
- Statue of Sir Henry May, 15th Governor of Hong Kong (1912–1918);
- A bronze statue of "Fame", the Hong Kong and Shanghai Bank's First World War memorial statue.[31]

---

[29] Hong Kong University of Science and Technology [13].
[30] Gwulo: Old Hong Kong [7].
[31] TAM Wing Sze [26], see also Gwulo: Old Hong Kong [8].

2.4 The Second World War

The Japanese also removed the pair of lions that stood outside the Hong Kong and Shanghai Bank Building on the south side of the Square. The Japanese also removed a statue from the Botanical Garden of Sir Arthur Kennedy, 7th Governor of Hong Kong (1872–1877). Kennedy was the first governor to have had a statue erected in Hong Kong, in 1887, some four years after his death.[32]

At the end of the War, the statue of Queen Victoria, the pair of HSBC lions, and the statue of Sir Thomas Jackson, 1st Baronet,[33] were the only statues to be recovered from Japan. The statue of Queen Victoria was re-sited at its present site in Victoria Park in Causeway Bay. The pair of lions were discovered in the Kawasaki Dockyard in Osaka and returned in 1946.[34] They now recline outside Norman Foster's Hong Kong and Shanghai Bank Building. Sir Thomas Jackson was returned as the sole bronze statue in Statue Square.

The Japanese did contribute to the built heritage of Hong Kong. They built various fortifications and military buildings which still stand today. Because of the difficult relationship Hong Kong has with its Second World War history, these are often not identified as Japanese. For example, as you enter Sai Kung in the east of the New Territories, on the main road from Pak Sha Wan, there is a building now used as the Lok Yuk Kindergarten. This building has fortified towers at each end. It was a private house, then used as the headquarters of the Japanese Kempeitai in this area during the War, then the site of the handover of Sai Kung back to the British by the East River Guerrillas, a temporary police station, a mission church and, since 1967, a kindergarten. The building was confirmed as a grade 2 historic building by the Antiquities Advisory Board on 4 March 2015 (Fig. 2.1).[35]

One well known contribution to Hong Kong's built heritage by the Japanese was the alteration to the Governor's House, now Government House. The Japanese carried out extensive conversion work, including the construction of a dominant central tower. After the War, the interior was restored to its former Western style but the tower remains.[36]

One noted Japanese addition to the built heritage of Hong Kong that was removed after the War was the Japanese War Memorial, sometimes referred to as the "Japanese Invasion Memorial," it was demolished on 26th Feb, 1947.[37]

---

[32] City Life Hong Kong: Enter the Irish [5].

[33] (1841–1915). The third Chief Manager of the Hongkong and Shanghai Banking Corporation. See Yanne and Heller [28].

[34] See South China Morning Post [24].

[35] Antiquities Advisory Board [2].

[36] AMO 59.

[37] Gwulo.com [6].

Fig. 2.1 Sai Kung Kindergarten

2.5 Continued Non-Legal Protection of Built Heritage in Hong Kong

After the Second World War, the focus in many jurisdictions was on rebuilding and concern for heritage was understandably not a priority. In Europe there was also a concern to eradicate any evidence of the Nazis, particularly sites associated with Hitler in order to prevent them becoming shrines. In Asia, there was less concern to eradicate evidence of the Japanese occupation, although their atrocities were no less than the Nazis. The tolerance of Japanese influence on the built environment was driven by economic necessity as the peoples of Asia did not have the luxury of resources to enable them to remove buildings erected during Japanese occupation. It was also driven by political necessity because the allies feared the rise of China in the region and so the policy towards Japan was arguably much more tolerant than to Nazi Germany. This tolerance extended to evidence of Japanese occupation on the built environment. Thus, as noted, some evidence of Japanese occupation still remains in Hong Kong today.

As the economy of Hong Kong recovered and prospered, new buildings were built in contemporary styles and also as tributes to the past. For the latter, in particular the banks and other institutions wishing to emphasise their permanence and power erected neo-classical tributes to wealth. For example, one of the most impressive historical bank buildings in Central is the Old Bank of China Building, dating from 1950.[38] However, these temples to commerce and finance in Hong Kong, as previously noted with the Hong Kong and Shanghai Bank Building, have tended to be regularly replaced to show the wealth and power of the organization.

The most important event in the post-war development of Hong Kong's built heritage protection policy was the discovery of a Han tomb at Lei Cheng Uk, Sham Shui Po, in 1955. The Tomb was discovered accidentally during work to level a hill to provide accommodation for resettlement of the homeless after the great fire in Shek Kip Mei.[39] As today, concerns about the opportunity cost of protecting heritage surfaced in debates at the time and the decision to preserve the Tomb was not popular with all sides, particularly with many in government, as the land had high development value. However, it was protected from looting by the prompt action of the Public Works Department, which also worked to conserve it, even if the method of concrete cladding may have actually damaged the structure.[40]

The discovery of the Lei Chen Uk tomb and the consequent stimulus for archaeological investigation and concern about protecting heritage during development formed the basis of the drive towards the main statutory development for the protection of cultural property and cultural heritage in Hong Kong—the Antiquities and Monument Ordinance.

2.6 The Development of the Antiquities and Monuments Ordinance

The Antiquities and Monuments Bill was first drafted in 1962, although it was being discussed in the late 1950s but was not presented to the Legislative Council until 1971.[41] The Ordinance was not implemented until 1976. Activist groups in Hong Kong had to fight against colonial government apathy and even hostility to gazette and commence the Ordinance.

Meacham claims justifiably that, "In large measure, the Antiquities and Monuments Ordinance (Cap 53) was developed because of concerns and pressure from archaeologists, in their desire to protect sites from pot-hunters and to preserve collections."[42] Thus, the main impetus was not to preserve built heritage but to protect archaeological sites. However, very soon activists with concern for built heritage

---

[38] South China Morning Post [23]. Return to its glorious past for Hong Kong's old Bank of China building in Central.

[39] The fire began on Christmas Eve 1953 and left nearly 6000 residents homeless. Multi Media Information System Hong Kong Public Libraries [17]. Stories of Hong Kong; for information on the Tomb see LCDS.gov.hk. [14].

[40] Meacham [15], at p. 11.

[41] Sinn [22], at p. 165.

[42] Meacham W. (2015) at p.13.

joined the campaign for legislation. Meacham has described the struggle to develop this legislation and much of the following is drawn from his work.[43]

Meacham notes that many in Hong Kong had long been concerned about the lack of protection for archaeological and other collections. Many of the valuable specimens collected in the pre-war era were kept in private collections and eventually lost. The Hong Kong government had little interest in these collections. Thus, one of the earliest and most valuable collections of archaeological materials amassed in Hong Kong, collected between 1926 and 34 by Henley and Shellshear,[44] was offered to the Hong Kong Government in 1938 but rejected and presented to the British Museum instead. Meacham notes this was fortunate with the benefit of hindsight as the collection might have fallen into the hands of the Japanese.[45]

The discovery of the Lei Chen UK tomb provided a focus for a campaign for legislation. The year after the discovery of the Lei Chen UK tomb, in 1956, the University Archaeology Team was formed at the University of Hong Kong, which began very soon pressing for protection of antiquities in Hong Kong by way of an antiquities ordinance. In 1967, the Team was dissolved to form the Hong Kong Archaeological Society. Of concern to the members of the Team and later the Society was not only the possible damage to archaeological sites during development but the seeming lack of care and protection that had been exhibited towards specimens that had previously been collected. A Bill for the preservation of historic relics was first drafted in 1962 and the Team promoted this and seemed to believe, as recorded in their records for 1964, that it would soon be law. However, the Chairman's Report for the Society in 1970 expressed disappointment that the Bill, pressed for since 1960, had not been made law. Meacham notes that the Society focused on the possible loss of relics rather than the loss of buildings, even though these, "were disappearing at a much faster pace than artefacts or archaeological sites."[46]

In 1971, with Sir David Trench in his final year as Governor of Hong Kong,[47] but now President of the Hong Kong Archaeological Society, the Bill was introduced to the Legislative Council. At its second reading Mr D.C.C. Luddington, Secretary for Home Affairs stated[48]:

"Sir, the purpose of this bill is to establish control over archaeological discoveries in Hong Kong and to ensure that items of particular historical interest are preserved for the enjoyment of the community. There has been a tendency in Hong Kong to concentrate on the needs of tomorrow rather than on preserving evidence of the past. Naturally this legislation will have to be very selective in its application so as to ensure that necessary developments are not held up for the preservation of antiquities of minor importance. We must however maintain a proper balance to

---

[43] Meacham W. (2015).

[44] The amateur geologist C.M. Heanley and Prof. Shellshear of the University of Hong Kong.

[45] Meacham W. (2015) at p.16.

[46] Meacham [16], at p.17.

[47] Governor of Hong Kong 1964–1971.

[48] Official Report of Proceedings of the Hong Kong Legislative Council, 3rd November 1971 [19], at p. 181.

ensure that future generations, while enjoying an improved environment, are able to learn something from worthy monuments of the past.

Clause 2 of the bill defined "relic" and "antiquity". Relics are defined as movable objects produced by human agency prior to the year 1800 A.D. and also fossils. Antiquities while including relics also mean structures and sites formed by human agency prior to 1800 A.D.

The emphasis upon "archaeological discoveries", "items of particular historical interest" and the definitions of "relics" and "antiquities" further evidence Meacham's identification of the origins of the Bill being archaeological concerns and activism. The choice of 1800 as a cut-off date was, as the Secretary for State later noted, "an arbitrary date chosen after considerable discussion."[49]

The emphasis on "selective" application with a "proper balance" for future generations also introduces the presumption that still operates in Hong Kong's approach to its heritage- the presumption that development and profit are more important than heritage.

Government hesitation regarding the balance between heritage preservation and development may have had much to do with the delay in implementation of the Act—gazetted at the end of 1971 but only implemented on 1st January 1976.

The concern for the built heritage of Hong Kong was only publicly raised in the 1970s and in particular in 1973 with concern about the possible future demolition of the Kowloon Canton Railway Station.

William Meacham notes the first building that raised his concern was the Old General Post Office Building in Central which was due for demolition in 1975—he states,

> It seemed a shame that this 'grand old lady' had to go, supposedly because the Central station of the underground mass transit railway had to be on that site. There were a few nostalgic objections raised in the press, but no one really protested strongly or made any effort to save her.[50]

The building was actually demolished in 1976, the same year the Antiquities and Monuments Ordinance went into effect. This was also the year that the colony's first pressure group to protect cultural property was born, the Hong Kong Heritage Society, because of the potential loss of another building, the Kowloon Canton Railway (KCR) Station. The KCR Station became the first built heritage to be considered under the provisions of the Antiquities and Monuments Ordinance.

References

1. Antiquities Advisory Board (2014) Respecting our heritage while looking ahead: policy on conservation of built heritage consultation paper, p 12. https://www.gov.hk/en/residents/government/publication/consultation/docs/2014/CBH.pdf. Accessed 8 June 2021

---

[49] Official Report of Proceedings of the Hong Kong Legislative Council, 17th November 1971 [20], at p. 218.

[50] Meacham W. (2015) at p.74.

2. Antiquities Advisory Board. 1,444 historic buildings and new items in addition to 1,444 historic buildings. One stop search for information on individual buildings. https://www.aab.gov.hk/historicbuilding/en/N96_Appraisal_En.pdf. Accessed 9 June 2021
3. Antiquities and Monuments Office. Introduction of archaeology. https://www.amo.gov.hk/scl/en/knowledge.php. Accessed 8 June 2021
4. Buildings Department website. New territories exempted houses. https://www.bd.gov.hk/en/safety-inspection/ubw/UBW-in-new-territories-exempted-houses/index_ubw_nteh_intro.html. Accessed 8 June 2021; see Buildings Ordinance (Application to the New Territories) Ordinance (Cap. 121)
5. City Life Hong Kong: Enter the Irish. https://web.archive.org/web/20100315192523/http://www.citylifehk.com/citylife/eng/history_0310.jsp. Accessed 8 June 2021
6. Gwulo.com. Japanese War Memorial: https://gwulo.com/japanese-war-memorial. Accessed 8 June 2021
7. Gwulo: Old Hong Kong. Details of statues in Statue Square. https://gwulo.com/atom/12948. Accessed 8 June 2021
8. Gwulo: Old Hong Kong: Fame, HSBC war memorial statue [1923–1942]. https://gwulo.com/node/7368#1/-20/242/Map_by_ESRI-Markers/100. Accessed 8 June 2021.
9. Historical Laws of Hong Kong Online. Chinese Temples Ordinance, 1928. https://oelawhk.lib.hku.hk/items/show/1606. Accessed 8 June 2021
10. Historical Laws of Hong Kong Online. Man Mo Temple Ordinance, 1908, section 2. https://oelawhk.lib.hku.hk/items/show/1235. Accessed 8 June 2021
11. Historical Laws of Hong Kong Online. Sung Wong Toi Reservation Ordinance, 1899. https://oelawhk.lib.hku.hk/items/show/1179. Accessed 8 June 2021
12. Home Affairs Bureau, Chinese Temples Committee, March 2015. Review on the Chinese Temples Ordinance Public Consultation Document. https://www.gov.hk/en/residents/government/publication/consultation/docs/2015/RCTO.pdf. Accessed 8 June 2021
13. Hong Kong University of Science and Technology. Three Years and Eight Months: Hong Kong during the Japanese Occupation. https://library.ust.hk/exhibitions/japanese-occupation/?page=Intro. Accessed 8 June 2021
14. LCDS.gov.hk. Lei Cheng Uk Han Tomb Museum. https://www.lcsd.gov.hk/CE/Museum/History/en_US/web/mh/about-us/lei-cheng-uk-han-tomb-museum.html. Accessed 8 June 2021
15. Meacham W (2015) The struggle for Hong Kong's Heritage—narrative, documents and reminiscences of the early years. Published by the Author, Hong Kong, p 4–11
16. Meacham W (2015) The struggle for Hong Kong's Heritage—narrative, documents and reminiscences of the early years. Published by the Author, Hong Kong
17. Multi Media Information System Hong Kong Public Libraries. Stories of Hong Kong. https://mmis.hkpl.gov.hk/shek-kip-mei-fire. Accessed 8 June 2021
18. Official Report of Proceedings of the Hong Kong Legislative Council, 16th June 1982, at p. 958: https://www.legco.gov.hk/yr81-82/english/lc_sitg/hansard/h820616.pdf. Accessed 8 June 2021
19. Official Report of Proceedings of the Hong Kong Legislative Council, 3rd November 1971, at p. 181. https://www.legco.gov.hk/yr71-72/h711103.pdf. Accessed 8 June 2021
20. Official Report of Proceedings of the Hong Kong Legislative Council, 17th November 1971, at p. 218: https://www.legco.gov.hk/yr71-72/h711117.pdf. Accessed 8 June 2021
21. Rose CM (1981) Preservation and community: new directions in the law of historic preservation. Stanford Law Review 33
22. Sinn E (1987) Modernization without Tears: attempts at cultural heritage conservation in Hong Kong. Paper presented at the symposium on cultural heritage and modernization held in Hong Kong 29 September-2 October 1987. Reprinted in full in Meacham W 2015 The struggle for Hong Kong's Heritage—narrative, documents and reminiscences of the early years Published by the Author Hong Kong Chapter 9
23. South China Morning Post. Enoch Yiu. 29 August 2017. Return to its glorious past for Hong Kong's old Bank of China building in Central. https://www.scmp.com/property/hong-kong-china/article/2108720/return-its-glorious-past-hong-kongs-old-bank-china-building. Accessed 8 June 2021

References

24. South China Morning Post. Gallagher, Steven. 19 December 2016. Hong Kong lions Stephen and Stitt, Japanese looters and the legal battle to protect cultural property. https://www.scmp.com/news/hong-kong/article/2055773/hong-kong-lions-stephen-and-stitt-japanese-looters-and-legal-battle. Accessed 8 June 2021
25. South China Morning Post. Mogul R. 3 July 2019. Hong Kong stories: The Indian immigrant who helped build HKU and the road that bears his name. https://www.scmp.com/yp/discover/lifestyle/features/article/3065557/hong-kong-stories-indian-immigrant-who-helped-build. Accessed 8 June 2021
26. TAM Wing Sze (2014) Public space and British colonial power: the transformation of Hong Kong Statue Square, 1890s-1970s. A thesis submitted in partial fulfilment of the requirement for the Degree of Master of Philosophy in History. Lingnan University. https://commons.ln.edu.hk/cgi/viewcontent.cgi?article=1004&context=his_etd. Accessed 8 June 2021
27. Wikipedia. Hong Kong Archaeological Society. https://en.wikipedia.org/wiki/Hong_Kong_Archaeological_Society. Accessed 8 June 2021
28. Yanne A, Heller G (2009) Signs of a colonial era. Hong Kong University Press, Hong Kong

Chapter 3
The Antiquities and Monuments Ordinance (Cap. 53)

Abstract The Antiquities and Monuments Ordinance may protect built heritage either by identification as antiquity or by declaration as proposed monument or monument. The definitions of antiquity restrict built heritage to pre-1800. The definition of a monument is more flexible as it provides a discretion for the Antiquities Authority to identify any site as a monument if it is of "historical, archaeological or palaeontological significance". If built heritage fulfils the criteria of an antiquity or declared a proposed monument or monument, then the Ordinance provides protection. This protection include powers for the Antiquities Authority and restrictions that on owners of land containing antiquities or monuments. As the declaration of a monument will restrict the occupiers and landowners use of the property and consequently its value, the Ordinance provides a process of objecting to the declaration and the payment of compensation to those landowners whose land may be adversely affected. In 1976, the Antiquities and Monuments Office and the Antiquities Advisory Board were established to assist the Authority and implement the Ordinance.

3.1 Introduction

As noted, the Ordinance was developed because of the discovery of a Han tomb at Lei Cheng Uk, Sham Shui Po, in 1955. It had its origins in the 1960s and was based upon similar provisions in England.[1] The Antiquities and Monuments Bill was presented to the Legislative Council in 1971 and gazetted at the end of the year. However, it was not commenced until 1976. At this time an Antiquities and Monument Section was created in the Urban Services Department to implement the Ordinances provisions and referred to as the Antiquities and Monuments Office (AMO). The Antiquities Advisory Board (AAB) was also established, under Section 17 of the Ordinance, in the same year, to assist the government in making decisions about matters involving the Ordinance, and to advise on assessing, conserving and preserving of antiquities.

---

[1] For example, the Town and Country Planning Act 1938, with amendments in 1944 and the subsequent Town and Country Planning Act 1968. See discussion in Legislative Council Secretariat IN26/07–08 [5].

The Antiquities and Monuments Ordinance provides for "the preservation of objects of historical, archaeological and palaeontological interest and for matters ancillary thereto or connected therewith."

It is worth emphasising that the Ordinance was drafted and commenced to protect archaeological sites primarily and was not intended to protect built heritage. Indeed, as Angus Forsyth has noted[2]:

> The background to the Antiquities and Monuments Ordinance (AMO) was the government's vision of a massive need in a place basically formed of mountains and with very little flat land to address the fast-growing priority requiring for high-rise property development. In the absence of developable land, this need was provided for by way of the physical destruction and redevelopment of existing build heritage into high rise.

Having noted this, the Ordinance may protect built heritage in two ways-first, under its default provisions if the built heritage is an antiquity or site containing relics, and second, by deliberate declaration of the built heritage as a monument.

3.2 Built Heritage as "Antiquity" or Site Containing "Relics"

The general provisions of the Ordinance extend to public and private land and include land held under lease, agreement for lease, tenancy agreement, license, permit, deed, or memorandum of appropriation, or other valid title from the government.[3] The Ordinance has provisions which deal with requirements to report discovery of relics and antiquities and sites on which these are found, and this provides protection for built heritage which has not been identified or declared as proposed monuments or monuments. The Ordinance provides penalties for those who do not comply with its requirement. For example there are penalties if a person does not report the discovery of a site which qualifies as an antiquity, knowingly makes "a false statement" about the discovery of an antiquity, excavates or searches for antiquities without a licence,[4] does not identifying an antiquity they have reported if so requested, and for wilfully obstructing the Authority, or any designated person authorized by him, in the exercise of his powers.[5] On conviction the offences carry maximum penalties of HK$5,000 and imprisonment for up to 6 months.

The Ordinance defines an "antiquity" as:

(a) a relic; and
(b) a place, building, site or structure erected, formed or built by human agency before the year 1800 and the ruins or remains of any such place, building, site

---

[2] Forsyth [4] at p. 176.

[3] Cruden [2].

[4] Including the use of metal detectors, as proscribed in Section 12aa.

[5] Antiquities and Monuments Ordinance (Cap. 53), Section 19.

or structure, whether or not the same has been modified, added to or restored after the year 1799.

Built heritage is most likely to fall within the definition of an "antiquity" under part (b) as, "a place, building, site or structure erected, formed or built by human agency before the year 1800 and the ruins or remains of any such". It is unlikely to fall with the definition of a relic as a "relic" is defined as:

(a) a movable object made, shaped, painted, carved, inscribed or otherwise created, manufactured, produced or modified by human agency before the year 1800, whether or not it has been modified, added to or restored after the year 1799; and
(b) fossil remains or impressions.

However, the site could contain relics and so get consequent protection under the Ordinance.

As Angus Forsyth has noted,[6] "given that Hong Kong was ceded to the United Kingdom in 1841, the AMO provides no recognition of antiquity in the buildings of the colonial period after 1841. Accordingly, the AMO takes no position on preservation of buildings from the colonial era."

Even if a building or site is identified as an "antiquity" in itself or a site containing "relics", it will usually only receive the protection of a reporting requirement. It is then up to the government to instigate full protection under the Ordinance by the declaration of the built heritage as a proposed monument or monument.

3.3 Built Heritage as "Monument" or "Proposed Monument"

If built heritage qualifies as an antiquity or site containing relics, it may be declared a monument or proposed monument. However, even if a building or site does qualify as an antiquity or site containing relics it may be declared a monument, and, of course, most of the buildings declared monuments in Hong Kong would not qualify as antiquities because of the 1800 cut-off. For example, the Old Marine Police Station in Tsim Sha Tsui was built in 1884.

The Ordinance provides that the Authority, presently the Secretary for Development,[7] may "declare any place, building, site or structure, which the Authority considers to be of public interest by reason of its historical, archaeological or palaeontological significance, to be a monument, historical building or archaeological or palaeontological site or structure."[8] The declaration is made in the Gazette.

---

[6] Forsyth [4] at p. 176.

[7] Antiquities and Monuments Ordinance, Section 2.

[8] Antiquities and Monuments Ordinance, Section 3.

The Ordinance defines a "monument" as, "a place, building, site or structure which is declared to be a monument, historical building or archaeological or palaeontological site or structure", by the Authority under their power in Section 3 of the Ordinance.[9]

The Authority must consult with the Antiquities Advisory Board when considering declaring a monument but does not have to follow their advice or gain their approval for any decision- whether he makes the declaration or not.[10] However, the Authority needs the Chief Executive's approval for declaration of a monument.[11]

The power to declare a proposed monument was added to the Ordinance in 1982 to provide provisional protection until a decision on the final designation of the building or site could be made.[12] The Authority may declare "any place, building, site or structure…a proposed monument, proposed historical building, or proposed archaeological or palaeontological site or structure".[13] The purpose of such declaration is to consider whether the place, building, site or structure should be declared a monument. The Authority does not need the approval of the Chief Executive to declare a proposed monument, but must consult the Antiquities Advisory Board, although, as with declaring a monument, the Authority does not have to follow the Board's advice.[14]

The Authority may declare a proposed monument for a maximum term of 12 months but may extend this period for a further 12 months for land not in private ownership with the approval of the Chief Executive.[15] The Authority may withdraw the declaration, allow it to lapse or declare the proposed monument a monument.

The Ordinance protects built heritage which has been declared as a proposed monument or monument by imposing a restriction on excavation and interference by way of a permit scheme.[16] The scheme prohibits, amongst other acts, the excavation, carrying on of building or other works, depositing earth or refuse on or in a proposed monument or monument, and the demolishing, removing, obstructing, defacing or interfering with a proposed monument or monument, except in accordance with a permit granted by the Authority. Such activities without permit are offences punishable on conviction with a maximum fine of HK$100,000 and imprisonment for up to 1 year.[17] Anyone refused a permit to carry out these acts may appeal

---

[9] Antiquities and Monuments Ordinance, Section 2.
[10] Antiquities and Monuments Ordinance, Section 2A(1).
[11] Antiquities and Monuments Ordinance, Section 3.
[12] Antiquities and Monuments Ordinance, Section 2A.
[13] Antiquities and Monuments Ordinance, Section 2A.
[14] Antiquities and Monuments Ordinance (Cap. 53), Section 2A (1).
[15] Antiquities and Monuments Ordinance, Section 2B.
[16] Antiquities and Monuments Ordinance, Section 6.
[17] Antiquities and Monuments Ordinance, Section 19(2).

3.3 Built Heritage as "Monument" or "Proposed Monument"

to the Chief Executive within 14 days of notice of the refusal by the Authority. The Chief Executive may confirm, vary or reverse the refusal.[18]

The Ordinance also empowers the Authority, with the prior approval of the Chief Executive, to authorise the fencing, repair, maintenance, preservation or restoration of any proposed monument or monument, and to excavate or search for relics in any proposed monument or monument and the removal of any relics thereby discovered.[19] These powers are limited when interfering with the property rights of owners or occupiers of the proposed monument or monument and require written permission from the Authority and his designated agents to enter the premises and restrict the Authority from excluding the owners from their land.[20]

3.3.1 Objection to Declaration as Monument or Proposed Monument

As the declaration of a proposed monument or monument restricts the use of property and consequently usually adversely affects the value of the property, there are objection policies for the owners or lawful occupiers of land within which the Authority intends to declare a monument or has declared a proposed monument.

The Authority has to serve on the owner and any lawful occupier of the private land a notice in writing of their intention to declare a monument on the land before they make the declaration.[21] The owner or lawful occupier then has a minimum of one month from the service of this notice to object to the intended declaration by petition to the Chief Executive. The Chief Executive may then direct that the intended declaration shall not be made or refer the objection to the Chief Executive in Council. If the objection is referred to the Chief Executive in Council, the Chief Executive may direct that:

(a) the intended declaration be made by the Authority in accordance with Section 3;
(b) the intended declaration be so made, subject to such variations or conditions as he thinks fit; or
(c) the intended declaration shall not be made.

A direction of the Chief Executive or of the Chief Executive in Council is final.[22]

---

[18] Antiquities and Monuments Ordinance, Section 6.
[19] Antiquities and Monuments Ordinance, Section 5(1).
[20] Antiquities and Monuments Ordinance, Section 5(2) & (3).
[21] Antiquities and Monuments Ordinance, section s.4.
[22] Antiquities and Monuments Ordinance, section s.4(6).

As the use of a declaration of a proposed monument is usually an emergency measure because of some threat to built heritage, for example by demolition, this is often a contentious matter and there is, again, an objection policy. The owner or any lawful occupier of private land within which a proposed monument has been declared may at any time apply to the Authority for withdrawal of the declaration.[23] The Authority must make a decision on this application within one month of the application either to withdraw the declaration or refuse the application. If the Authority decides to refuse the application the owners may object by petition to the Chief Executive.[24] The Chief Executive may direct that the declaration stands, vary the declaration, or direct that it be withdrawn. The Authority's and Chief Executive's decisions are final and not open to review by the courts, as noted in the attempt to review the Authority's decision regarding the refusal to declare the Queen's Pier a proposed monument.[25]

Having declared a proposed monument, the Authority will within the designated period make a decision to either remove the proposed monument status or declare it a monument. This declaration requires consultation with the Board as before, and the approval of the Chief Executive.[26]

3.3.2 Compensation for Declaration as Monument

As previously noted, the declaration of a monument restricts the use of property and consequently usually adversely affects the value of the property, therefore the Ordinance provides for the paying of compensation to the owner or lawful occupier of monuments. However, this payment is discretionary and not a right, and requires the approval of the Chief Executive.[27] There are two other grounds for compensation: first, the Authority entering onto private land for inspection, or to fence, repair, maintain, preserve or restore the monument or to search or excavate for relics; and, second, the Authority refusing to grant a permit for the carrying on of building or other works. However, there will be no grounds for compensation if the financial loss has been or may be suffered in connection with a contract made or anything done by the owner or lawful occupier after they have been given notice of the intention to make a declaration.[28] If the Authority decides to exercise their discretion with the approval of the Chief Executive to pay compensation then that should be as agreed

---

[23] Antiquities and Monuments Ordinance, section s.2C.
[24] Antiquities and Monuments Ordinance, section s.2C (3).
[25] *Chu Hoi Dick and another v Secretary for Home Affairs* [2007] 4 HKC 263.
[26] Antiquities and Monuments Ordinance, section s.3.
[27] Antiquities and Monuments Ordinance, Section 8.
[28] Antiquities and Monuments Ordinance, Section 8(3).

3.3 Built Heritage as "Monument" or "Proposed Monument"

with the owner, or as assessed by the District Court.[29] If the owner does not agree with the proposed amount then they may apply to the District Court for assessment.[30] There have been no applications for assessment made to the District Court at the time of writing.

Although the power to pay compensation is discretionary, and it therefore seems that the owner has no real recourse apart from accepting the compensation offered or appeal to the Chief Executive, there may be other routes available to land owners for compensation if they are not satisfied. There may be a claim under Hong Kong's mini-constitution, the Basic Law. This provides in Basic Law 6, that the Hong Kong Special Administrative Region shall protect the right of private ownership of property in accordance with law. This is supported by Basic Law 105, which provides that the Hong Kong Special Administrative Region shall, in accordance with law, protect the right of individuals and legal persons to the acquisition, use, disposal and inheritance of property and their right to compensation for lawful deprivation of their property. Such compensation shall correspond to the real value of the property concerned at the time and shall be freely convertible and paid without undue delay.[31] Thus, any "lawful deprivation" of their property should be compensated- it would be up to the courts to consider whether the blanket refusal to interfere in the Authority's and the Chief Executive's discretionary use of their powers under the Ordinance would apply to compensation calculations.[32]

If all else failed, the land owners could try rallying public support by the time-honoured means of noting that if their property rights can be restricted, so can everyone else's-something that is bound to attract attention and concern if not sympathy in property obsessed Hong Kong.

3.4 Antiquities and Monuments Office

The administration of the Antiquities and Monuments Ordinance is under the purview of the Leisure and Cultural Services Department (LCSD), together with its executive arm, the Antiquities and Monuments Office (AMO). The Antiquities and Monuments Office was set up at the same time that the Antiquities and Monuments Ordinance came into effect in 1976. It was created in the Urban Services Department to implement the Ordinance's provisions. The Executive Secretary of the Section was appointed in October.

---

[29] Antiquities and Monuments Ordinance, Section 8(2).
[30] Antiquities and Monuments Ordinance, Section 9.
[31] Department of Justice [3].
[32] *Chu Hoi Dick and another v Secretary for Home Affairs* [2007] 4 HKC 263.

The Antiquities and Monuments Office is responsible for the enforcement of the provisions in the Antiquities and Monuments Ordinance and so the day-to-day operation of the protection and preservation of Hong Kong's archaeological and built heritage. This includes assessing the condition of sites and buildings and conducting rescue excavations of archaeological sites under threat from development. It also assists the Development Bureau in its partnership schemes by processing and assessing adaptive reuse applications. The Office is therefore responsible for the protection of Hong Kong's declared monuments. At the time of writing, 9 June 2021, there are 126 Declared Monuments in Hong Kong.[33] There is a diverse range of examples of built heritage which have been recognised by declaration including rock carvings, forts, lighthouses, temples, the Hong Kong Observatory, police stations and even the Duddell Street granite steps and gas lamps (Fig. 3.1).

Hong Kong's public heritage building conservation projects are mainly undertaken by the Home Affairs Bureau, where the Antiquities and Monuments Office is situated, although the Development Bureau and other government offices, departments and officials may be involved. Such projects can involve the Government buying out the private owner's legal title of the land and building or doing a land swap with the owner. The actual conservation and restoration work of monuments and historic buildings is carried out by the Architectural Services Department, under the Works Branch of the Development Bureau this is responsible for works on Government-owned and Government-funded facilities. From 2008, the government has taken a more creative approach to conservation projects, implementing the Revitalizing Historic Buildings through Partnership Scheme, which we will consider later.

The Antiquities and Monuments Office is also the secretariat of the Antiquities Advisory Board.

3.5 Antiquities Advisory Board (AAB)

The Antiquities Advisory Board was also formed in 1976. Its main purpose is to aid in the identification of heritage which needs declaratory protection. The Antiquities Advisory Board met for the first time in January 1977. The members are unpaid citizens appointed by the Chief Executive. The Antiquities Advisory Board's duties are restricted to advising the Antiquities and Monuments Office and ultimately the Authority on decisions for declaring monuments and proposed monuments. It has no powers. It has adopted an administrative grading system to aid in deciding which buildings should be declared monuments, but this has no legal effect. The grading system is discussed below.

---

[33] Antiquities and Monuments Office [1].

3.5 Antiquities Advisory Board (AAB)

Fig. 3.1 Duddell Street granite steps and gas lamps

References

1. Antiquities and Monuments Office. Declared Monuments in Hong Kong. https://www.amo.gov.hk/en/monuments.php. Accessed 9 June 2021

2. Cruden G (2009) Land compensation and valuation law in Hong Kong, 3rd edn. LexisNexis, Hong Kong
3. Department of Justice. Protection of Property Rights under BL 6 and BL 105. https://www.doj.gov.hk/en/publications/pub20030002_i12.html. Accessed 9 June 2021
4. Forsyth A (2020) Hong Kong. In: Kaye L, Spiegler H (eds) The art law review. The Law Reviews, London
5. Legislative Council Secretariat IN26/07–08. Information Note. Built heritage conservation policy in the United Kingdom. https://www.legco.gov.hk/yr07-08/english/sec/library/0708in26-e.pdf. Accessed 9 June 2021

Chapter 4
Problems with the Antiquities and Monuments Ordinance Pre-1997

Abstract After implementing the Ordinance the colonial government tried its best to ignore it. This was not possible as a number of high profile cases arose where the people of Hong Kong objected to the proposed loss of their built heritage. The government did its best to progress with its policy of building new and erasing the old in the face of popular opposition. This resulted in the loss of important built heritage, notably the Kowloon Canton Railway (KCR) Station in Tsim Sha Tsui. However, the government did make an important amendment to the Ordinance in 1982, to include the power to declare proposed monuments as an emergency measure. The government used this power to declare the Ohel Leah Synagogue a proposed monument in 1987, but then rescinded the declaration permitting development, which was only avoided fortuitously. In the last decade of colonial rule, the realisation that Hong Kong was shortly to cease being a British colony did speed up the process of declaring monuments, particularly those of the colonial era. However, the colonial government faced a final built heritage issue- the public concern at the reclamation of land from the Victoria Harbour, an issue that has continued to the present day.

4.1 Introduction

Almost immediately after it was implemented, the shortcomings of the legislation were being identified. The focus of heritage protection in Hong Kong was identified in the initial appointments to the Antiquities and Monuments section, for example Dr Solomon Bard was its first executive secretary (1976–1983), and was mainly interested in archaeology.[1] Thus built heritage was not a major concern of the Antiquities and Monuments Office, which was largely seen by the beginning of the 1980s as a "rubber stamp" for government policy.[2] Such were the immediate problems with regard to built heritage, that it is apparent that the colonial government intended the legislation to permit development and removal of heritage. Indeed, as Angus Forsyth has noted, in its quest for more living space for an increasing population, "…from the early 1970s, the Hong Kong government encouraged the demolition of the often

---

[1] Antiquities and Monuments Office [4].
[2] Meacham [9] at p. 38.

century-old built heritage of Hong Kong of usually one-, two-, or three-storey brick and granite buildings and their replacement by huge new concrete structures...".[3]

The colonial government's disregard for the colonial built heritage of Hong Kong is highlighted by high profile cases involving public campaigns to save buildings. For example, the Hong Kong Heritage Society fought and lost a battle to preserve the Kowloon Canton Railway (KCR) Station in Tsim Sha Tsui from 1976 to 1978. This was followed by the campaign led by local archaeologist and activist William Meacham to preserve the Ohel Leah Synagogue on Robinson Road from 1980–1989, which was financially and emotionally bloody for those involved but, fortunately, ultimately successful. As Meacham notes, "What was entirely missing in the introduction and early application of this law was the necessary attention to historical buildings; that only happened with the rise of the Heritage Society and the public pressure it generated."[4]

4.2 Hong Kong Heritage Society 1976–1984

The Hong Kong Heritage Society developed from a group of concerned Hong Kong residents who began meeting in 1976. This group had received information from a source within the Urban Council[5] with details of a plan which had been devised in 1974 to demolish the Kowloon Canton Railway (KCR) Station[6] and the Marine Police Headquarters Compound[7] in Tsim Sha Tsui and to level the hill on which the Police Headquarters stood. The site would then be used for "a modern cultural complex with open space and park", an enlarged bus terminus and a multi-storey building.[8] In November 1976 the plan was made public and protests began. The Antiquities Advisory Board discussed the development and recommended the clock tower and façade of the station be declared as a monument under the Antiquities and Monuments Ordinance. However, there were influential members of the government who were determined to remove the KCR Station. In particular Meacham notes the lack of independence in the bodies considering the development and making recommendations to those responsible for decisions under the Ordinance. For example, Brian Wilson was the chair of the Urban Council committee making decisions on development, the chair of the Antiquities Advisory Board advising the Authority with the designating powers to declare monuments, and the Antiquities Authority

---

[3] Forsyth [8] at p. 176.

[4] Meacham [9] at p. 18.

[5] Founded as the Sanitary Board in 1883, renamed the Urban Council in legislation in 1936, replaced by the Provisional Urban Council in 1997 and dissolved on 31st December 1999. The operations of the Urban Council are now subsumed within two newly created government departments: The Food and Environmental Hygiene Department and the Leisure and Cultural Services Department.

[6] Constructed 1912–16: The Industrial History of Hong Kong Group [14]. The Kowloon-Canton Railway (British Section) Part 3—the construction of Kowloon Station.

[7] Constructed in 1884.

[8] Meacham [9] at p. 3.

himself, as acting Secretary for Home Affairs. Thus, he had to advise himself in both previous capacities on the decision and had the power to make the declaration. Thus, Wilson held multiple advisory roles and ultimate we rot make the declaration, although he had expressed on several occasions determination to demolish all evidence of the KCR Station.[9]

The Hong Kong Heritage Society was officially formed in April 1977 and had its first public meeting at St John's Cathedral ion 22 June 1977 with over 100 people present.[10] By November 1977 the Hong Kong Heritage Society had gathered 14,360 signatures to support its petition for the government to preserve the station and the clock tower, which, the Society noted, was "about double the turnout for the Urban Council elections".[11] At the same time the Society began campaigning for more public consultation for the planned development of the Victoria Barracks in Admiralty, Hong Kong Island.[12]

In February 1978 after the government's announcement that it would continue with its plans to redevelop the KCR Station site, the Society petitioned the Queen to ask her to intercede. Unfortunately, the response came from the Hong Kong government in the form of a polite letter of refusal. The KCR Station was demolished shortly after with only the clock tower remaining.[13] However, the original plans to demolish the Marine Police Headquarters Compound and level the hill on which it stood were not carried out and today this site has been preserved, in controversial fashion, as Heritage 1881.

4.3 Monument Declarations to 1984

The use of the declaratory powers in the Antiquities and Monuments Ordinance was slow and sporadic. Only nine monuments had been gazetted by the end of 1980, with only two of these being "historical buildings", including the Duddell Street Gas Lights, and none being privately owned. This latter observation reflecting the concerns about affecting property rights and values.[14] The government was particularly concerned about affecting property rights and potential development profits and so refused to exercise its power under the Ordinance to declare monuments for a number of high profile buildings. For example, the Hong Kong Club building, built in 1898, was recommended as a monument by the Antiquities Advisory Board but was turned down by the governor in council in 1980, and the building was demolished

---

[9] Meacham [9]. See discussion in Chap. 6.

[10] Digital Repository @HKUL [7].

[11] Other groups also expressed concern, for example the Kowloon Residents' Association wrote to the Colonial Secretary in 1970, and the Tsim Sha Tsui Neighbourhood and Welfare Association wrote to the Colonial Secretary in 1975 and1977. See Sinn [10].

[12] Constructed between the 1840s and 1874.

[13] Meacham [9] at p. 79.

[14] Sinn [10] at p. 160.

in 1981. It may be that, as with many governments and their use of legislation, the colonial Hong Kong government thought that by introducing legislation to protect heritage they had apparently fulfilled their promised policy and did not have to comply with it.

Other challenges to the declaration of monuments included infighting within the government bureaucracy itself. For example, the government backed down on plans to declare a monument of the Lei Chen UK tomb, when the museum authority controlling it at that time claimed this was unnecessary interference.[15] The tomb was finally gazetted as a monument in 1988.[16]

In the early 1980s, the Antiquities Advisory Board was criticised by the Heritage Society for having "no teeth", as it was merely advisory and was often disregarded by the Authority. The members of the Board took this criticism seriously and so requested the government to provide the Board with a block vote fund to use to encourage private owners of buildings which the Board believed had heritage merit and should be preserved to preserve them and not to object so vehemently to monument status. The Board also proposed a similar listing system for sites and buildings as was used in the United Kingdom to offer wider protection. The block vote fund was introduced but the listing proposal was never introduced.[17]

There were some cases where public opinion was motivated to force the government to change its plans and save built heritage, although not always by preserving it where it stood. In 1981 plans were announced to demolish Murray House in Central.[18] The Antiquities Advisory Board had recommended declaring this as a monument, and Sinn notes that the Board fought hard to protect it.[19] The government would not declare it a monument or protect it where it stood, as the site was promised to the Bank of China. Instead a plan was announced to relocate the building. The building was dismantled in 1982; all parts were labelled and stored and the building was rebuilt at Stanley in 2002.[20]

Also in 1982, the power to declare a proposed monument as an emergency measure to protect a site was added to the Authority's powers in the Antiquities and Monuments Ordinance.

However, public activism concerning built heritage receded as Hong Kong had more pressing matters to consider.

---

[15] Meacham [9] at pp. 109–110.

[16] https://www.lcsd.gov.hk/CE/Museum/History/en_US/web/mh/about-us/lei-cheng-uk-han-tomb-museum.html.

[17] Sinn [10] at p. 159.

[18] Built in 1844 as the officers' quarters of the Murray Barracks.

[19] Sinn [10] at p. 165.

[20] Stanley Market. Murray House [12].

4.4 Sino-British Joint Declaration of 1984

The most important event for Hong Kong in the 1980s was the announcement of the Sino-British Joint Declaration of 1984. This announced that Hong Kong would cease to be a British colony and returned to China on 1 July 1997.[21] Although the Declaration guaranteed a 50 year period to 2047 of "One Country, two Systems", Sinn, writing in 1987, noted this was a particularly fateful announcement for built heritage conservation in Hong Kong because, as the clock ticked towards 1997, all tried to make their profits as quickly as possible, and there was "even less inclination to indulge in luxuries such as conservation."[22] Thus, there was little concern in government or the governing commercial sector for the protection of built heritage. As Teather and Chow noted, the announcement reinforced the perception that Hong Kong was a temporary place.[23] This was followed by the Tiananmen Square protests in 1989 which provoked horror and apprehension among Hong Kong's residents. It was no surprise that emigration from Hong Kong peaked in 1992 at around 75,000–80,000. Many considered that Hong Kong had been given an end date. Happily, for many, they were mistaken and the handover was not so much of a change as they feared.

With such gloomy thoughts for the future of Hong Kong, it is still reassuring that there were some willing to fight to protect built heritage to pass on to the future residents of Hong Kong, including the most famous campaign of the 1980s, the campaign to preserve the Ohel Leah Synagogue.

4.5 Ohel Leah Synagogue 1985–89

In Meacham's words,

> This was without doubt the greatest battle that has ever been fought in Hong Kong over a heritage issue. The Heritage Society's struggle to preserve the KCR station a few years previously was almost the same duration in time but did not generate as much sustained publicity, infighting within the community and on the AAB, plus general bitterness.[24]

The Ohel Leah Synagogue was built in Robinson Road and completed in 1902. The Synagogue and the land it stands on were held subject to a charitable trust created in 1903, with more land entrusted in 1937. In 1980 the trustees sought court consent to vary the terms of the trust. At the same time the trustees incorporated under the name, "The Incorporated Trustees of the Jewish Community of Hong Kong." The trustees wanted to vary the terms of the trusts as they claimed that they no longer had the funds to repair and maintain the original building. Therefore, they would

---

[21] 19 December 1984.
[22] Sinn [10] at p. 165.
[23] Teather and Chun [13].
[24] Meacham [9] at p. 176.

seek to develop the site. The Attorney General should have been joined to all court proceedings involving charitable trusts but declined to join these proceedings. In 1982, a tentative agreement was signed between the trustees and Hong Kong Land to redevelop the site to include two 37-storey buildings above a 4-storey podium, this was discussed with members of the congregation. A news article appeared in the South China Morning Post on October 18, 1985, reporting on the development plan, and immediately drew expressions of concern. Falling land prices meant that Hong Kong Land withdrew from the agreement and Swire Properties negotiated a new arrangement. However, many members of the Jewish community in Hong Kong were concerned and they sought guidance on Jewish law regarding the proposed demolition of the Synagogue from the Chief Rabbi of London and the Chief Rabbis of Israel. The general advice to the trustees from the Jewish authorities in Israel was that the planned demolition if not against Jewish law was at least immoral. A concern group was formed to try to prevent the development called simply "Save Our Synagogue Committee" or "SOS".

Pressure came from this group and the public generally to reopen the legal questions regarding the trust and press for the Antiquities Advisory Board to propose the Synagogue a monument and so protect it. This last proposal met support internally as the Board had been reorganised to remove most civil servants and replace them with archaeologists (including William Meacham), anthropologists, historians and professionals. However, Meacham notes there were internal disputes in the Board as some wished to protect government interests.

Swire applied for a demolition order for the Synagogue in May 1987, and the government unexpectedly responded by declaring the Synagogue a proposed monument on 4 July. This was the first time the government had used this emergency power. Hong Kong's press now began to lobby strongly for protection of the building. However, at the end of December, before the one year proposed monument status would expire, the proposed monument status was revoked.

In 1988 the issue of development split public opinion in Hong Kong and on the Antiquities Advisory Board. In April 1988 Meacham launched a judicial review of the Antiquities Authority's failure to make an unfettered decision in line with the legislation.[25] However, the trustees of the Synagogue and Swire Properties applied to be joined to the proceedings which made the possible legal costs extortionate if Meacham lost and he had to withdraw his review application. In May the Chief Rabbi of London advised that the Synagogue could be demolished as this was not against Jewish law.

However, in April 1989, the trustees announced that the Synagogue would not be demolished but would be restored. It seems the problems associated with finding a replacement synagogue during development for the congregation who were strict orthodox Jews meant the Synagogue could not be demolished. For example, any replacement synagogue had to be within walking distance because of the prohibition of taking transport on the Sabbath.

---

[25] At that time the Secretary for Municipal Services.

4.5 Ohel Leah Synagogue 1985–89

Although the heritage campaigners had indirectly succeeded, there was fallout from the victory and many of those involved are still bitter at what they regarded as underhand and dirty tricks played by the colonial government and the Trustees of the Synagogue. Meacham was tactically removed from the Antiquities Advisory Board and a few years after the Board returned to the appointment process which effectively placed all members under government control. The Government Ombudsman investigated some of the allegations of misstatement and collusion against government officials involved in the decision making and advice on the Synagogue's fate and found some serious issues with their conduct- some of these government personnel were then promoted and received honours.[26]

A new renovation project for the Synagogue was undertaken in 1998. In 2000 the trustees of the Synagogue received a UNESCO Asia Pacific Heritage Award for Cultural Heritage Conservation for this renovation project. The Antiquities and Monuments Office noted, "Not only did the Synagogue preserve its integrity and use as a Jewish communal place, it also partook a very positive contribution to architectural conservation in Hong Kong and Asia."[27] This award was made to the expressed disgust of some of the campaigners who noted these trustees included some who had intended to demolish the Synagogue. However, perhaps we should celebrate converts and their redemption.

4.6 The New Territories in the 1980s and 1990s

The New Territories contains much of the oldest built heritage in Hong Kong. For example, the Rock Inscription at Joss House Bay, dated 1274,[28] and the Tin Hau Temple in front of this rock, which is said to date from 1266. Interestingly, the rock inscription was one of the first declared monuments in Hong Kong, in 1979, but the Temple has never been declared a monument, although the Antiquities Advisory Board have recognised it as a Grade I Historic Building. Perhaps as the Temple is administered by the Chinese Temples Committee and subject to relevant legislation, it is thought unnecessary to declare it a monument for further protection.[29]

A problem for the built heritage of the New Territories was a privilege the British administration afforded the indigenous residents. This privilege was part of the special treatment which has been given to the indigenous residents of the New Territories. This special treatment led to one colonial administrator, Austin Coates, famously describing the indigenous of the New Territories as "China's spoiled children."[30] Coates referred to them in this way because of the special emphasis that the British had paced on recognising local custom in the laws of Hong Kong only for

---

[26] Meacham [9]. Chapter 12.

[27] Antiquities and Monuments Office [3].

[28] AMO 04.

[29] Chinese Temples Committee [5].

[30] Coates [6] p 62.

these residents. In heritage terms this impacted and still impacts today as the colonial and post-colonial governments have been wary of interfering in any way with the property rights of the indigenous residents of the New Territories. This has led to the contentious Small House Policy, introduced by the British administration in 1971, and which may or may not be a customary right, and a reluctance to interfere with land held by indigenous residents or by their customary trust associations, the *t'ong* and *t'so*, which hold land for burial, religious, educational and social purposes for the benefit of male clan members.

This land-holding in the New Territories is often a heritage issue in itself, as Hong Kong is the only jurisdiction in the world to recognise in its legal system these Chinese customary trusts for land, and these only in the New Territories. These are mostly in the form of the *t'ong* and *t'so* trust structures. These Chinese customary trusts control much of the land upon which temples, ancestral clan halls, scholar buildings and graves are situated. Many of the most important heritage buildings in the New Territories are held subject to these clan trusts and the colonial government in particular was wary of interfering with the rights of these groups, not least because of the political power of these groups in Hong Kong. In the 1980s concerns were raised about the lack of protection afforded many of these examples of built heritage, as the indigenous peoples of the New Territories had been leaving behind their rural existence and seeking opportunity by migrating to the city areas or new towns, or even emigrating since the 1960s. Thus, villages were abandoned and their old buildings left to deteriorate.[31] In the 1990s, the built heritage of the New Territories faced a reversal of this problem from an influx of residents. As transport to these rural areas improved and the cost of living in the city areas and new towns increased, public and private developments were undertaken in the space of the New Territories to the loss of built heritage.

However, there have been examples of clan groups making sacrifices of opportunity to profit from development by the decision to permit or even suggest the gazetting of their buildings as monuments. For example, the Tang Clan have permitted the gazetting of many buildings which now form the Ping Shan Heritage Trail. The Trail was instituted in 1993, although the majority of the buildings were gazetted in 2001.[32] In fact the majority of buildings declared monuments in the 1980s and early 1990s were ancestral properties in the New Territories. Thus, of the 39 declared monuments in Hong Kong by the end of 1989, 20 are in the New Territories. Of these, 7 are archaeological sites including rock inscriptions and ruins, 12 are ancestral-linked properties, and only two are colonial buildings.[33]

---

[31] For example, Sham Chung, Sai Kung West Country Park, see *South China Morning Post*. 12 March 2016 [11].

[32] It should be noted this required "generous financial support" from the Jockey Club and Lord Wilson Trust. Antiquities and Monuments Office [2].

[33] Island House and the Old District Office North.

4.7 Declared Monuments in the Run-Up to "The Handover"

Having noted the slow progress of declarations of monuments by the colonial government in the early 1980s and the focus on ancestral properties in the New Territories and archaeological sites elsewhere in Hong Kong, the early 1990s saw a significant number of colonial buildings and sites being declared monuments. The number of declared monuments increased from 39 at the end of 1989 to 64 in January 1997. Of these 25 declarations, 17 were of colonial era buildings, many significant to the colonial administration. For example, in 1994 the old Marine Police Headquarters Compound in Tsim Sha Tsui, the subject of public anger in the 1980s, was finally declared a monument, and the Governor's residence, referred to as "Government House" after the handover, was gazetted as monument in 1995.[34].

This focus on protecting built heritage closely linked to the colonial regime by declaration of monuments may have been because of concerns that the new administration would seek to erase evidence of the British colonial era.

A further positive was the announcement that the Antiquities and Monuments Office with the assistance of the Antiquities Advisory Board would begin a territory-wide survey of built heritage in 1996.[35] This would continue until its report in 2000. However, there was pubic concern about the most famous aspect of built heritage in Hong Kong- the Victoria Harbour.

4.8 The Last Colonial Built Heritage Issue-Victoria Harbour

Victoria Harbour is the reason for Hong Kong. It was the deep natural harbour that the British coveted and gained from the First Opium War, and it was the source of Hong Kong's initial success and continued prosperity till late in the twentieth century. An image of the Victoria Harbour is usually the first image anyone will think of when they think of Hong Kong. However, the harbour is not all natural, over the last 180 years it has been subject to much alteration by dredging and reclamation of land, and is arguably the largest and most evident aspect of Hong Kong's built heritage. In November 1995, because of concerns about plans for further reclamation of the Victoria Harbour, the Society for Protection of the Harbour (SPH) was formed. The Society ran the "Save Our Harbour" Campaign in 1996 which amassed 170,000 signatures from the Hong Kong public and succeeded in opposing the Government's proposal of reclaiming 190 hectares (20.5 million square feet) of Green Island. In June 1996, The Protection of the Harbour Bill was presented to the Legislative Council by Christine Loh as a private members' bill. The Bill was gazetted on 27 June 1997

---

[34] AMO 59.
[35] Antiquities and Monuments Office website [1].

as the Protection of the Harbour Ordinance, Cap. 531. As subsequently noted, the Ordinance recognises that "the harbour is a special public asset and a natural heritage of the Hong Kong people".[36]

References

1. Antiquities and Monuments Office website. Historic Buildings in Hong Kong. https://www.amo.gov.hk/en/built.php. Accessed 9 June 2021
2. Antiquities and Monuments Office. Heritage Trails. http://www.amo.gov.hk/en/trails_pingshan.php. Accessed 9 June 2021
3. Antiquities and Monuments Office. Historic Building Appraisal: https://www.amo.gov.hk/form/brief_information_grade1.pdf. Accessed 9 June 2021
4. Antiquities and Monuments Office. Obituary Dr Solomon Matthew Bard, OBE, ED, JP (1916–2014). http://www.amo.gov.hk/en/whatsnew_20141120.php. Accessed 9 June 2021
5. Chinese Temples Committee. Administered Temples. http://www.ctc.org.hk/en/directcontrol/temple20.asp. Accessed 9 June 2021
6. Coates A (1976) Myself a Mandarin: Memoirs of a Special Magistrate. Heinemann Educational Books (Asia) Ltd., Hong Kong, p 62
7. Digital Repository @HKUL. Hong Kong Heritage Society Archives. https://digitalrepository.lib.hku.hk/hkhsa#?xywh=-236%2C37%2C2257%2C2257 Accessed 9 June 2021
8. Forsyth A (2020) Hong Kong. In: Kaye L, Spiegler H (eds) The Art Law Review. The Law Reviews, London
9. Meacham W (2015) The Struggle for Hong Kong's Heritage—narrative, documents and reminiscences of the early years. Published by the Author, Hong Kong
10. Sinn E (1987) Modernization without tears: attempts at cultural heritage conservation in Hong Kong. Paper presented at the symposium on cultural heritage and modernization held in Hong Kong 29 September-2 October 1987. Reprinted in full in Meacham W 2015 The Struggle for Hong Kong's Heritage—narrative, documents and reminiscences of the early years Published by the Author Hong Kong Chapter 9
11. South China Morning Post. 12 March 2016. Windows into the past: see inside the abandoned villages of Hong Kong. https://www.scmp.com/magazines/post-magazine/travel-leisure/article/1922844/windows-past-abandoned-villages-hong-kong. Accessed 9 June 2021.
12. Stanley Market. Murray House. http://www.hk-stanley-market.com/Murray-House/#.XAjqMfZuJMs. Accessed 9 June 2021
13. Teather E, Chun S (2003) Identity and Place: the testament of designated heritage in Hong Kong. Int J Heritage Stud 9(2):93–115. Available via https://www.tandfonline.com/doi/abs/10.1080/13527250304772. Accessed 9 June 2021.
14. The Industrial History of Hong Kong Group. The Kowloon-Canton Railway (British Section) Part 3—the construction of Kowloon Station. https://industrialhistoryhk.org/kowloon-canton-railway-british-section-3-kowloon-station/. Accessed 9 June 2021.

---

[36] *Town Planning Board v Society for Protection of the Harbour Ltd* (2004) 7 HKCFAR 1.

Chapter 5
The Hong Kong SAR and Built Heritage 1997–2006

Abstract Post-colonial Hong Kong initially seemed to be very positive towards its built heritage, even the colonial heritage. The first Chief Executive extolled the value of heritage in the 1999 Policy Address and the Urban Renewal Authority was established with one of its considerations for development being to "preserve buildings, sites and structures of historical, cultural or architectural interest". A local think-tank, Civic Exchange, produced a critical Report in 2002, which recommended a number of measures to ensure Hong Kong's built heritage was protected. Shortly after, the post-colonial government instituted the second declaration of a proposed monument for the Morrison Building and subsequently made the first declaration of a monument for this building in opposition to the owner. The government followed this by purchasing Kom Tong Hall, to prevent it being developed. Most significantly, the Antiquities and Monuments Office's concluded its Territory-wide Survey of Historic Buildings, with publication of those identified as of heritage merit using their grading system. However, there were some negatives with regard to the government's heritage policy with allegations of corruption in the Antiquities and Monuments Office and continued problems because of plans for the reclamation of parts of Victoria Harbour.

5.1 Introduction

The first ten years of Hong Kong's post-colonial government heritage policy started well and ended disastrously. If anyone had expected the post-colonial government to be more aware of the importance of heritage now that Hong Kong was again part of China, they were sorely disappointed. Although one concern was not realised.

This was the concern that with the handing back of the British Colony of Hong Kong to the Peoples' Republic of China in 1997, the new government might understandably distance Hong Kong from its colonial past, as had happened in many former colonies, by removing evidence of colonial buildings. It seemed this would be more likely in Hong Kong, as it was restored to a resurgent China. As noted, the colonial government had seemingly tried to forestall this by declaring a number of significant colonial buildings as monuments in the run-up to the handover. However, this concern was unnecessary, as there was no widespread renaming of building, streets and districts, no removal of colonial statues and no destruction of colonial buildings, well no more than was usual in Hong Kong.

In fact, the return of Hong Kong to China and the establishment of the Hong Kong Special Administrative Region of China was initially accompanied with signs that built heritage would be recognised and protected.

5.2 Positive Signs for Built Heritage Protection

There was a series of positive indications for the future of built heritage in Hong Kong in the first few years of the new government. For example, in October 1999, the Chief Executive, Tung Chee Hwa, in response to pressure from the Society for Protection of the Harbour, promised in his 1999 Policy Address to downsize the reclamation plan for the Harbour and to follow the principle of sustainable development. He also noted the importance of preservation as an objective for sustainable development and heritage tourism:

> It is important to rehabilitate and preserve unique buildings as this not only accords with our objective of sustainable development but also facilitates the retention of the inherent characteristics of different districts, and helps promote tourism...... Hong Kong possesses a unique cultural history going back several thousand years. This not only helps us to establish our identity but also serves to attract tourists.[1]

The Policy Address was followed, in November 1999, by the extension of the geographic coverage of the Protection of the Harbour Ordinance, which originally applied only to the area of the Harbour around Central, to the entire area of Victoria Harbour.[2]

Other notable events which were interpreted as positive for heritage protection included the establishment of the Urban Renewal Authority, the Civic Exchange "Saving Hong Kong's Heritage" Report, the second use of "Proposed Monument" declaration for the protection of the Morrison Building in 2003, the consequent first declaration of a building as a monument in the face of opposition from a private owner for this building in 2004, the government purchase of Kom Tong Hall to protect it from development, and, most significantly, the conclusion of the Antiquities and Monuments Office's territory-wide survey of historic buildings in Hong Kong.

5.2.1 The Urban Renewal Authority

In 2001, the Urban Renewal Authority Ordinance (Cap 563) was implemented which established the Urban Renewal Authority (URA) to replace the Land Development Corporation. The URA is a statutory quasi-government corporation which may

---

[1] Hong Kong Chief Executive [6].
[2] Harbour-front Enhancement Committee [5].

embark upon renewal projects by financing these either alone or with private persons. The Ordinance provides that the Secretary for Development, "may prepare from time to time an urban renewal strategy for the purposes of ... carrying out of urban renewal."[3] In preparing this strategy, the Secretary for development "shall consult the public before finalizing the urban renewal strategy", although this consultation may be in "in such manner as he may determine."[4]

The Ordinance lists one of the purposes of the URA is to "preserve buildings, sites and structures of historical, cultural or architectural interest".[5] On its website the URA claims it fulfils this purpose through "Heritage Preservation and Revitalisation."[6] The Authority has been involved in a number of heritage related preservation projects, many of which, have been criticised. However, it should be remembered that the Authority's main purpose is to alleviate the terrible housing conditions of many of Hong Kong's residents, with heritage preservation one of six stated purposes, and thus, arguably, a minor concern.

5.2.2 Civic Exchange "Saving Hong Kong's Heritage" Report, 2002

In February 2002 a report was published from the Civic Exchange think-tank,[7] entitled, "Saving Hong Kong's Heritage",[8] with the following key recommendations:

- "Establish a dedicated conservation authority at the highest decision making level to develop and apply consistent heritage conservation principles. This body needs to ensure the efficient co-operation of existing government and non-government conservation bodies and the ongoing provision of funds for the implementation of conservation efforts;
- Formulate and adopt a heritage conservation policy. This legally-backed policy needs to include strategies to alleviate threats to conservation and benchmarks to measure progress;
- Develop mechanisms to promote private sector participation in heritage conservation. These mechanisms must recognize existing economic forces in order to develop tools which promote sensitive land development and protection of heritage assets;
- Push initiatives that encourage general public involvement in heritage conservation. These initiatives should identify community values, promote education and

---

[3] Urban Renewal Authority Ordinance, Section 20(a).
[4] Urban Renewal Authority Ordinance, Section 20(b).
[5] Urban Renewal Authority Ordinance, Section 5(e).
[6] Urban Renewal Authority [9].
[7] Civic Exchange describes itself as is an independent, non-partisan public policy think-tank established in Hong Kong in 2000. Civic Exchange [4].
[8] Chu and Uebegang [3].

develop consensus-building processes which involve genuine public contribution to policy formulation and decision-making;
- Improve the effective operation of its existing ordinances and administrative bodies" including:

1. improvements to existing ordinances such as an extension of protection to incorporate all areas and districts, building types, and other intangible heritage assets, creation of zoning categories which provide for the protection of heritage assets, inclusion of heritage conservation as a "public purpose," requirement for housing projects to undergo environmental impact assessments, and inclusion of heritage considerations in the New Territories Small House Policy;
2. Improvements to the operation of existing conservation related bodies, including a revision of existing grading systems to ensure protection of buildings beyond those that are "monumental quality", increased resources to reduce the backlog of sites under consideration for protection, creation of mechanisms to identify heritage sites within the town planning process, proper maintenance of government-owned vacant heritage sites and development of a tourism management system and guidelines.

The Report contained the following conclusion:

Decision-makers have tended to systematically overlook issues of conservation, especially when pitted against the short-term economic incentives of modernisation. However, with open debate and a willingness to address concerns, it should be possible to derive an effective strategy that incorporates the needs and concerns of all stakeholders. This report was written in this spirit of constructive cooperation.

The Report was greeted with some optimism for the future protection of Hong Kong's heritage. However, all concern for heritage was overshadowed in Hong Kong by the terrible severe acute respiratory syndrome (SARS) epidemic between November 2002 and 2003. The report resulted in little or no change to heritage policy, although it has been referred to in subsequent debate about issues that have arisen because these recommendations have not been implemented.

5.2.3 The Second "Proposed Monument" Declaration: Morrison Building, 2003

This period saw the second use of the "proposed monument" status for a building and the first declaration of a monument in the face of opposition from a private owner. The Morrison Building in the Hoh Fuk Tong Centre in Tuen Mun was originally part of a villa built in 1936 by General Cai Tingkai (1892–1968). He was a member of the Nineteenth Route Army, a force renowned for its brave resistance against the Japanese invasion.[9] The building is also important as,

---

[9] AMO 79.

5.2 Positive Signs for Built Heritage Protection

From 1946 to 1949, it was turned into the Dade Institute - a tertiary education institution founded under the directive of Chinese leaders Zhou Enlai and Dong Biwu.... The building bears witness to the unique role played by Hong Kong in the history of modern China and the establishment of the People's Republic.[10]

The government had been negotiating with the private owners since 2001 trying to protect the building while permitting development of the rest of the site. In March 2003 the owner applied for a demolition permit and in April the government announced the proposed monument status. The government declared it a monument a year later in 2004.

5.2.4 Proposed Development of Kom Tong Hall, 2002–4

Kom Tong Hall is a distinctive classical dwelling built in 1914 in the Mid-levels of Hong Kong Island. It was one of the first buildings in Hong Kong with a steel frame and concealed electrical wiring and was built in a distinctive Greek-style with granite columns, wrought iron balconies and red-brick walls. It was built by Ho Kom-tong (1866–1950) a wealthy Euro-Chinese merchant as his family home. The Ho name is significant in Hong Kong's history of built heritage issues and protection as Ho was the younger brother of Sir Robert Ho Tung, who we will consider later with regard to the controversy over his property, Ho Tung Gardens. In 1960 the family sold the property to a Chinese merchant who sold it in 1961 to the Church of Jesus Christ of Latter-day Saints. In 2002 the Church announced plans to demolish the building for development. The local community protested against this destruction. The government responded to public pressure and, in 2004, after a lengthy negotiation with the church, paid HK$53 million to the church to acquire the mansion. It is now a memorial museum for Dr Sun Yat-sen.[11]

5.2.5 Antiquities and Monuments Office's Territory-Wide Survey of Historic Buildings

Most significant for built heritage protection in Hong Kong, in 2000, the Antiquities and Monuments Office finished the territory-wide survey of old buildings in Hong Kong. This had begun in 1996 and focused mainly on those built before 1950, with over 8800 buildings recorded. Between 2002 and 2004, a more in-depth survey was conducted of 1444 buildings with higher heritage value selected from the 8800 surveyed buildings.[12] To assist their work, the Antiquities Advisory Board and the

---

[10] Hong Kong Government Press release [7].
[11] AMO 98.
[12] Antiquities Advisory Board [1].

Antiquities and Monuments Office developed their own administrative guidelines for the protection of historic buildings. The Grades were defined as[13]:

- Grade I–Building of outstanding merit for which every effort should be made to preserve if possible;
- Grade II–Building of special merit; which efforts should be made to selectively preserve; and
- Grade III–Buildings of some merit, but not yet qualified for consolidation as possible monuments. These buildings are to be recorded and used as a pool from which future monuments may be selected.

5.3 Problems for Built Heritage Under the Post-Colonial Government

These promising signs for the protection of built heritage in Hong Kong were then followed by a series of threats to the built heritage which caused strong reaction from its residents much to the bemusement of the government. Initially the issues were the usual for Hong Kong and many jurisdictions—administrative corruption, incompetence, apathy and broken promises, but the cumulative effect was to ferment violent protest.

5.3.1 Allegations of Corruption in the Antiquities and Monuments Office, 2002

In the early 2000s, the Antiquities and Monuments Office was rocked by allegations of corruption. The allegations stemmed from the recruitment of four teams of mainland archaeologists for a salvage archaeology excavation at Sha Ha in Sai Kung. This was,"the largest, most expensive and most publicised archaeological excavation ever carried out in Hong Kong at that time."[14] The decision to bring in mainland teams was criticised for many reasons but eventually led to allegations of corruption and the two most senior Antiquities and Monuments Office officials were arrested in 2002 for corruption. One was never charged. One was convicted and then acquitted on appeal.

---

[13] Antiquities and Monuments Office [2].
[14] Meacham [8] at p. 57.

5.3.2 Continued Problems for Victoria Harbour

Despite the Chief Executive's promises and comments about sustainable development in his 1999 Policy Address, the government continued with its reclamation plans for the Victoria Harbour. As noted, the SARS epidemic overshadowed all concerns for heritage until early 2004. When things regained some normality the pressure groups began reminding the government of its promises. The Society for Protection of the Harbour used legal means, such as judicial review to try to prevent some of the reclamation projects in the Harbour area.[15] In addition, they organised protests. The judicial reviews were ultimately unsuccessful in preventing reclamation although they did identify important principles. In particular, the decision of the Court of Final Appeal in January 2004 in ***Town Planning Board v Society for Protection of the Harbour Ltd***.[16]

The Court was unanimous in its judgment. The Court construed Section 3 of the Protection of the Harbour Ordinance as providing the purpose of the legislation was to ensure that the Harbour will be protected against excessive reclamation. Thus, there was a statutory presumption against reclamation. This did not mean that the Town Planning Board could just consider not reclaiming the Harbour, it had to consciously decide whether the presumption had been rebutted. The Court then considered what would be sufficient to rebut this presumption developing the "overriding public need test". Therefore, the presumption may only be rebutted by establishing an overriding public need for reclamation. These public needs would include economic, environmental and social needs of the community and would only be regarded as overriding if they were a compelling and present need. The Court noted a compelling and present need goes far beyond something which is "nice to have", desirable, preferable or beneficial. However, it does not have to be in the nature of a last resort, or something which the public cannot do without. The Court also noted that where there was a reasonable alternative to reclamation, an overriding need for reclamation would not be made out. Further, it would be necessary for each proposed area of reclamation to be justified separately. The Court referred the decision back to the Board to take note of the test.

The Society for Protection of the Harbour urged the Government to halt all reclamation works in Central Reclamation Phase III and asked the Town Planning Board to conduct a proper review of their plans with regards to the "overriding public need test". In March, the Society for Protection of the Harbour held the "Hand-in-Hand" Rally in which over 10,000 people formed a "human chain" along the Harbour from Central to Wan Chai to demonstrate against harbour reclamation. The Board reconsidered its decision in light of the "overriding public need test" and justified further reclamation.

In 2005, the Society for Protection of the Harbour organised further public campaigns to protest against the reclamations. From April to May, it held the "Kids

---

[15] For example, *Town Planning Board v Society for Protection of the Harbour Ltd* (2004) 7 HKCFAR 1.

[16] (2004) 7 HKCFAR 1.

Love the Harbour Campaign" and the "Giordano selling Saving Victoria T-shirt" for teenagers. In September, the "Victoria Harbour and I" Photo Competition was held. In November, the Action Group on Protection of the Harbour and Friends of the Harbour joined together for the first time to launch the Harbour Week Carnival at the Golden Bauhinia Square, Wan Chai, to encourage people to appreciate and care for the Victoria Harbour. However, reclamation and development continued.

5.4 Conclusion—1997–2006

Thus the period 1997 to 2006 had started with positive signs for heritage protection in Hong Kong but the governments early statements of support for built heritage protection were soon ignored even in the face of strong public opposition to development, except in the case of Kom Tong Hall and the Morrison Building, which arguably were saved as they represented a relatively small opportunity cost for the government compared to abandoning the development plans for the Victoria Harbour.

However, the government was about to face the most important public challenge to its development plans, which, although it did not save the built heritage in question, would force the government into its most significant concessions for future heritage policy.

References

1. Antiquities Advisory Board (2005) Frequently asked questions on assessment of buildings in Hong Kong which may have heritage value. https://www.aab.gov.hk/form/AAB_brief_faq_en.pdf. Accessed 9 June 2021
2. Antiquities and Monuments Office. March 2009 publication of the assessment of 1,444 historic buildings. http://www.amo.gov.hk/en/built2.php. Accessed 9 June 2021
3. Chu C, Uebegang K (2002) Civic exchange report. Saving Hong Kong's Heritage. Available via saving Hong Kong's cultural Heritage—Civic exchange (civic-exchange.org) Accessed 9 June 2021
4. Civic Exchange. Our Mission. http://www.civic-exchange.org/en/about-us/our-mission. Accessed 9 June 2021
5. Harbour-front Enhancement Committee. Harbour-Front Enhancement Review—Wan Chai, Causeway Bay and Adjoining Areas ("HER"). Paper No. 2/2004. Protection of the Harbour Ordinance and the Court of Final Appeal Judgment. https://www.harbourfront.org.hk/eng/content_page/protection.html?s=1. Accessed 9 June 2021
6. Hong Kong Chief Executive: The 1999 Policy Address. Paragraphs 133 and 164. https://www.policyaddress.gov.hk/pa99/english/espeech.pdf. Accessed 9 June 2021.
7. Hong Kong Government Press release. 18 March 2004. "Historic Morrison Building to become a monument": https://www.info.gov.hk/gia/general/brandhk/0318003.htm. Accessed 9 June 2021
8. Meacham W (2015) The Struggle for Hong Kong's Heritage—narrative, documents and reminiscences of the early years. Published by the Author, Hong Kong
9. Urban Renewal Authority. Heritage Preservation & Revitalisation. https://www.ura.org.hk/en/heritage-preservation-and-revitalisation. Accessed 9 June 2021

Chapter 6
Heritage and Social Unrest: 2006–7

Abstract The first 10 years of Hong Kong's post-colonial government's heritage policy, which had started seemingly more positive than the colonial government's, ended disastrously in 2006. This was the year that Hong Kong's people fought for their built heritage with violent protests at the Star Ferry Pier in Central to try and prevent its demolition. These protests were unsuccessful but protestors continued to try and prevent the demolition of the Queen's Pier in 2007. Such was the strength of public opinion and protest that the government did concede that they would not demolish the Queen's Pier but dismantle it and rebuild it in the new development of the Victoria Harbour. Further, the Urban Renewal Authority was criticised for ignoring its duty to consider heritage with its commercial development of Wedding Card Street. To round off a tumultuous 2007, the government was forced to make an emergency declaration of a proposed monument to prevent the demolition of King Yin Lei. However, this was more a response to public outcry than a sign of the government's positive commitment to built heritage, as details emerged of the government's previous failure to negotiate with the owner to protect the building.

6.1 Introduction

The year 2006–7 is notable in Hong Kong's history as the year the people of Hong Kong fought for their heritage, some of them literally. The government faced such a major backlash against its development plans and perceived disdain for built heritage, that it had to, begrudgingly, develop new protection. Nearly 30 years after the public protest at the demolition of the KCR terminus near the Star Ferry in Tsim Sha Tsui, the Hong Kong SAR government faced even more protests over their removal of the Star Ferry and Queen's Pier in Central. The two piers were not the only built heritage issues in this period. There was also public concern and criticism over the renovation of Lee Tung Street (Wedding Card Street) in Wan Chai by the Urban Renewal Authority, and the initial failure of the government to protect King Yin Lei.

6.2 Star Ferry and Queen's Pier

The plan to demolish the Star Ferry and Queen's Pier had been agreed in government since the handover in 1997 and announced shortly after. Arguably it is understandable that the government may have underestimated the strength of feeling that the removal of the piers generated as they were both relatively modern construction and of dubious architectural merit—except to fans of brutalist 1950s concrete architecture. The Star Ferry was built in 1957 and the Queen's Pier in 1954. The latter was not even the original structure, but the second pier structure built along newly reclaimed waterfront.[1] The original announcements of the plans did not attract much opposition. In particular, it could be argued that the Queen's Pier, named after Queen Victoria, no longer had any purpose to fulfil as Hong Kong ceased to be a British colony. This was because it had been used as the main ceremonial arrival and departure point for vising British colonial officials. These included all Hong Kong's governors since 1925 and, most notably, Queen Elizabeth II in 1975, and Prince Charles in 1989.[2]

The government had announced the Star Ferry and Queen's Pier would be dismantled as part of a process of massive land reclamation from the Harbour on the Hong Kong Island side. In 2001 the government commissioned an Environmental Impact Assessment (EIA) Study as part of the reclamation project which was designated "Central Reclamation Phase III". As part of this assessment a heritage impact assessment was conducted, which recommended the relocation of the piers in line with government plans but did note that the Star Ferry pier should be preserved for its "great significance".[3] The assessment was not made fully available to the public until it was leaked by a pressure group on 11 December 2006, as the pier was being demolished.[4] Long before this, in 2000, the Antiquities and Monuments Office commissioned a consultant to conduct a survey on the removal of the structures.[5] The Survey noted that the Star Ferry was an important landmark in Hong Kong as well as an impressive tourist attraction though not a historical building because of its year of construction (1957). The Survey noted the Star Ferry had long been a site of protests, a hunger strike at the pier on 5 April 1966 was one of the triggering events of the riots of 1966, the worst in Hong Kong's history.[6] The Survey recommended that the Clock Tower be relocated, if not the whole pier building, to a new suitable area in harmony

---

[1] The original structure was a wooden pier known as "Queen's Statue Wharf", which was replaced by a concrete and steel pier which was situated roughly where Pedder Street now is and which was named "Queen's Pier" in honour of Queen Victoria on 31 July 1924. It was demolished in January 1955 as part of post-war land reclamation. See Chai [3], p. 85.

[2] Lu [6].

[3] Hong Kong Government Press releases. Legislative Council Question 14. December 6, 2006 [5].

[4] See South China Morning Post [9].

[5] A Survey Commissioned by the Antiquities and Monuments Office, Leisure and Cultural Services Department (February 2001), para 5.12 [1].

[6] Lai C. South China Morning Post [10].

6.2 Star Ferry and Queen's Pier 63

with its "ambiance".[7] As Meacham notes, it was "perspicacious"[8] in concluding that the removal of the Star Ferry pier would "likely raise public objection and dismay".[9]

6.2.1 Star Ferry 2006

When the people of Hong Kong realised that the removal of these landmark piers was imminent their reaction shocked and unsettled the government. In the light of the opposition to the development of the Victoria Harbour and the Antiquities and Monuments Office's commissioned survey, it may be argued it should not have. Criticism of the failure to protect the sites had already been made and the consequent outpouring of nostalgia was mixed with public protest. Over 150,000 people watched the last day of the Star Ferry's operation from the pier and attempted to ride on these last historic sailings on 11 November 2006. Over 1,800 people paid HK$88 or 40 times the normal fare for the last ride, with proceeds going to charity.[10] On 19 November, protestors began a sit-in at the pier to protest at the relocations and were joined by So Sau Chung, the hunger striker whose protest had triggered the 1966 riots. On 13 December police moved in to evict protestors and some were "dragged off kicking and screaming by police".[11] On December 14, a large group gathered to celebrate the pier's 49th birthday but ended up clashing violently with police and a number of arrests were made. The clock tower was dismantled in the early hours of 16th December 2006.[12] The pier was demolished in January 2007. Public opinion was further incensed by stories being reported of the old materials of the clock tower and pier being unceremoniously destroyed at landfill sites.[13]

6.2.2 Queen's Pier 2007

The public protests against the destruction of the Star ferry had some limited success in changing the government's policy for the Queen's Pier. Because of the force of public opinion, particularly with regard to the destruction of the fabric of the Star Ferry pier, it was proposed in the Legislative Council, on 21 March 2007, that the Queen's Pier be dismantled and reassembled at a new site. However, the protestors were still arguing that in-situ preservation was possible. The government argued this

---

[7] Antiquities Advisory Board Press Releases [2].

[8] Meacham [7] at p. 273.

[9] A Survey Commissioned by the Antiquities and Monuments Office, Leisure and Cultural Services Department. (February 2001) [1].

[10] New York Times [8].

[11] Chai [3], p. 57.

[12] South China Morning Post [10].

[13] Chai [3], p. 58.

would result in unacceptable costs and delays, particularly with regard to the Hong Kong Airport train link, estimating that the extra cost might be HK$500 million and take more than two years to complete.[14]

On 26 April 2007, the Queen's Pier was closed for its demolition as part of the reclamation plan. The closing of the Pier aroused fierce opposition by conservationists. There were calls for the Pier to be declared a monument under the Antiquities and Monuments Ordinance and thus ensure its protection. The Antiquities Advisory Board (AAB) held a public hearing on 9 May, and Board members voted a 'Grade 1' listing for the Pier by a majority.

On 22 May 2007 the Secretary for Home Affairs, at that time the Antiquities Authority, announced the decision not to declare the Queen's Pier a monument. Activists filed for a judicial review of the Secretary for Home Affairs' decision. On 29 July, Secretary for Development Carrie Lam Cheng Yuet-ngor repeated the government's insistence that keeping the Pier was not an option. She said she would "not give the people false hope".[15]

On 1 August, 2007, amongst heated protest, police officers evicted 30 protesters from the site. The Court of First Instance hearing for the judicial review began on 7 August and was dismissed on 10 August The Court ruled that the Antiquities Authority's decision was legal, it had discretion not to declare the Pier a monument, and agreed that the Authority should adopt a high threshold in declaring a monument in line with past practice. In effect the decisions of the Chief Executive and Antiquities Authority were final and not amenable to judicial review.[16] On 17 August work began on dismantling the Pier. The Queen's Pier was dismantled completely by February 2008 and its base piles removed in March 2008. The outcry about its rebuilding and re-siting continues today.[17]

6.3 Wedding Card Street and the Urban Renewal Authority 2007

The 2007 redevelopment of Lee Tung Street (also known as Wedding Card Street) and McGregor Street, an area covering 8,900 square meters in Wan Chai, also drew criticism.

Although the Urban Renewal Authority Ordinance mandates public consultation, this had been seriously lacking for this project. The URA spent HK$3.58 billion demolishing buildings and replacing them with four high-rise buildings, an underground car park, and new shops that together made up the image of a wedding city. The project was most heavily criticized for putting business considerations before community. Most of the residents accepted compensation to move from the area but

---

[14] The Standard [12].

[15] The Standard [13].

[16] *Chu Hoi Dick and Ho Loy v Secretary for Home Affairs* HCAL 87/2007.

[17] South China Morning Post [11].

some formed a pressure group to object to the plans, with some even engaging in hunger strikes. However, their protests were largely ignored. The heritage buildings were gone including the famous tenement block, the *tong lau*, which had occupied the middle of the street, to be replaced by a shopping mall.

6.4 King Yin Lei 2007

King Yin Lei is a traditional courtyard house built in 1937 with a blend of Chinese and Western design elements.[18] As it was built by a prominent Chinese on the Peak at a time when Chinese were still subject to restrictions in their free movement on the Peak and their right to live there other than as servants was debatable, the property has huge social and historical value for Hong Kong. In 2004 the original family owning the building sold it. In 2007 the new owner of the building began its demolition.[19] The owner later stated this was because he had asked the government if they were interested in the building and had received no favourable reply. Indeed, it seems likely that the owner intended to draw public attention to help save the building. For example, workmen began using power tools to remove decorative elements from the roof rather than just using a wrecking ball to attack the whole fabric of the building. The demolition attracted protest. The government made the third ever use of proposed monument designation to protect it on 15 September 2007. It was subsequently declared a monument on 11 July 2008. The Chief Executive in Council then approved a non-in-situ land swap for the site of the building.[20] As Meacham notes, the valuable land was precisely what the owner wanted in the first place and had tried to negotiate from the government initially.[21] However, only by starting to destroy the building and attracting public attention and outcry could he get the government to act (Fig. 6.1).

6.5 Conclusion—2007

Although the colonial government and post-colonial governments have generally adopted a refusal to concede to public protest in Hong Kong, the post-colonial government was shocked by the strength of public opposition to the loss of built heritage evidenced in 2006–7. This shock translated onto some major and some cosmetic changes to heritage policy in Hong Kong.

---

[18] Yeung [14].
[19] AMO 85.
[20] Conserve and Revitalise Hong Kong Heritage [4].
[21] Meacham [7] at p. 279.

Fig. 6.1 King Yin Lei

References

1. A Survey Commissioned by the Antiquities and Monuments Office, Leisure and Cultural Services Department (February 2001) A Survey Report of Historical Buildings and Structures within the Project Area of the Central Reclamation Phase III: https://www.epd.gov.hk/eia/register/report/eiareport/eia_0552001/report/vol2/eia_0552001appendix_w.pdf. Accessed 9 June 2021
2. Antiquities Advisory Board Press Releases. AAB reaffirms no objection raised to Star Ferry Pier demolition plan in 2002. https://www.info.gov.hk/gia/general/200612/12/P200612120263.htm. Accessed 9 June 2021.
3. Chai K. (2009) Central Star ferry pier: policy, politics and protest in the making of heritage in Hong Kong. Thesis for PhD at the University of Hong Kong. Available via The HKU Scholars Hub. http://hub.hku.hk/bitstream/10722/152558/1/FullText.pdf
4. Conserve and Revitalise Hong Kong Heritage. Batch III of Revitalisation Scheme. https://www.heritage.gov.hk/en/kyl/background.htm. Accessed 9 June 2021
5. Hong Kong Government Press releases. Legislative Council Question 14. December 6, 2006. Rating of historical buildings. www.info.gov.hk/gia/general/200612/06/P200612060159.htm. Accessed 9 June 2021
6. Lu T (2009) Heritage conservation in post-colonial Hong Kong. Int J Herit Stud 15:258–272
7. Meacham W (2015) The struggle for Hong Kong's Heritage – narrative, documents and reminiscences of the early years. Published by the Author, Hong Kong, At p, p 273
8. New York Times. Ng T. 10 November 2006. Not even HK's storied Star Ferry can face down developers. https://www.nytimes.com/2006/11/10/world/asia/10iht-ferry.3482674.html. Accessed 9 June 2021
9. South China Morning Post, Lai C. 12 December 2006. 2001 report backs preservation of Star Ferry pier
10. South China Morning Post. Lai C. 17 December 2006. Curse of the Star Ferry pier. https://www.scmp.com/article/575779/curse-star-ferry-pier. Accessed 9 June 2021
11. South China Morning Post. Leng S. 9 March 2016. Queen's Pier resurrected? Hong Kong officials considering design options near its former site. https://www.scmp.com/news/hong-kong/economy/article/1922668/queens-pier-resurrected-hong-kong-officials-considering. Accessed 9 June 2021
12. The Standard. Chong W. 22 March 2007. New spot for pier at old location
13. The Standard. Una So. 30 July 2007. Death knell on pier

References

14. Yeung H (2012) Heritage in Hong Kong-city with/without history. J Depart Plan Archit UWE: 58–61. https://www2.uwe.ac.uk/faculties/FET/news/publications/Project2012.pdf. Accessed 9 June 2021

Chapter 7
The Government's Heritage Concessions

Abstract After a year of protest, the Hong Kong government was forced to make concessions and commit to more protection for built heritage. This began by the concession to dismantle rather than demolish the Queen's Pier, and the commitment to rebuild it in the future development of the Victoria Harbour. The role of Antiquities Authority was passed to the Secretary for Development with a commitment to heritage preservation. The Chief Executive's Policy Address 2007 announced major reforms and initiatives for built heritage protection including the establishment of a Commissioner for Heritage's Office, the requirement for Heritage Impact Assessments for all capital projects and the initialisation of the Revitalizing Historic Buildings through Partnership Scheme. In addition, the Hong Kong government threw itself into the identification and celebration of Hong Kong's intangible cultural heritage.

7.1 Introduction

The government had been disconcerted by the public opposition to the the loss of their heritage in 2006–2007-particularly by the violent protests at Star Ferry and Queen's Pier. The initial reaction of the government to the Star Ferry protests seemed just lip service to heritage conservation. Chief Executive Donald Tsang, in his 28 January 2007 Letter to Hong Kong on RTHK, told citizens: "Your insistence in preserving these buildings signifies the recognition of personal identity and the sense of belonging to Hong Kong." He said he was "touched by the sincerity of the emotions expressed by people who are not represented by any well-established group or political party." However, although he promised to "keep pace with public sentiment" on heritage issues, he also noted: "We cannot afford heritage preservation if we do not preserve our economic sustainability".[1] Shortly after this he was re-elected and oversaw the removal of the Queen's Pier in direct opposition to strongly expressed public opinion. However, again, there was some concession in the promise to dismantle, store and relocate the Queen's Pier, rather than demolish it. At the time of writing (June 2021) this is a promise that has still not been honoured.

---

[1] South China Morning Post [7].

However, the further protests at Queen's Pier, the public criticism of the redevelopment of Lee Tung Street (Wedding Card Street) in Wan Chai by the Urban Renewal Authority, and the failure of the government to protect King Yin Lei until its owner had begun its demolition, were important factors leading to true concessions by the government to try to appease public anger. These concessions took the form of policy changes, new initiatives, and a commitment to more consultation with the public about developments that affect heritage and heritage protection generally.

7.2 The Secretary for Development-The Antiquities Authority

The first major change was the designation of a new Antiquities Authority. The Authority had been the Secretary for Home Affairs but on 1 July 2007, the Housing, Planning and Lands Bureau was re-formed into the Development Bureau. The Department's portfolio included heritage alongside land, planning and public works. The Secretary for Development became the Antiquities Authority for the Antiquities and Monuments Ordinance. The Department's policy statement on heritage conservation says this role is[2]:

> To protect, conserve and revitalize as appropriate historical and heritage sites and buildings through relevant and sustainable approaches for the benefit and enjoyment of present and future generations. In implementing this policy, due regard should be given to development needs in the public interest, respect for private property rights, budgetary considerations, cross-sector collaboration and active engagement of stakeholders and the general public.

This change was followed by the Chief Executive's Policy Address, which instead of merely mentioning heritage protection as desirable, devoted an entire section to heritage conservation and positive commitments.

7.3 Chief Executive's Policy Address 2007

In the Chief Executive's Policy Address of October 2007 new initiatives were announced intended to protect Hong Kong's built heritage. Donald Tsang announced a series of administrative measures including[3]:

- The creation of a Commissioner for Heritage Office to support the Secretary for Development in implementing heritage conservation policy and the initiatives announced in the policy address;
- The commitment that public works projects would have to undergo a heritage impact assessment in the planning stage;

---

[2] Conserve and Revitalize Hong Kong Heritage [1].
[3] Donald [4].

7.3 Chief Executive's Policy Address 2007

- The introduction of a new scheme whereby government-owned historic buildings would be leased at nominal rent to NGOs for adaptive reuse as social enterprises, with $1 billion earmarked to help them revitalise the buildings within professional conservation standards so that they could retain their heritage values;
- The provision of economic incentives to encourage private owners of historic properties to conserve them would be "explored", and financial support to maintain privately owned graded historic buildings offered.

7.3.1 The Commissioner for Heritage's Office

On 25 April 2008 the Secretary for Development set up the Commissioner for Heritage's Office under the Development Bureau. The Office's purpose is "to provide dedicated support to Secretary for Development in implementing the policy on heritage conservation and keeping it under constant review, taking forward a series of new initiatives on heritage conservation and serving as a focal point of contact, both locally and overseas."[4] The Office's roles include:

1. to conduct heritage impact assessments for new capital works projects;
2. to implement the Revitalizing Historic Buildings Through Partnership Scheme for Government-owned historic buildings;
3. to provide economic incentives for conservation of privately owned historic buildings;
4. to facilitate maintenance of privately owned graded historic buildings; and
5. to take forward conservation and revitalisation projects.

7.3.2 Heritage Impact Assessments

The Policy Address promised that heritage impact assessments would be carried out for all public projects. These are conducted under the statutory power and guidance in the Environmental Impact Assessment Ordinance (EIAO) (Cap 499), which was implemented in 1998. The policy was implemented by the Technical Circular (Works) No. 6/2009 "Heritage Impact Assessment Mechanism for Capital Works Projects" as promulgated by the Development Bureau.[5] All Government capital works now require a heritage impact assessment at the project planning stage before development may begin with the devising of mitigation measures and a commitment to public engagement.[6]

---

[4] Conserve and Revitalize Hong Kong Heritage [1].

[5] Development Bureau [3].

[6] In accordance with the Technical Circular (Works) No. 6/2009 [8]. Heritage Impact Assessment Mechanism for Capital Works Projects. Antiquities and Monuments Office. Heritage Impact Assessments.

The Ordinance specifies in its Technical Memorandum that heritage impact assessments (HIA) should be carried out at the early planning stage of any required development. The EIAO specifies in Schedule 1 Interpretation that "environmental impact" for a designated project includes an on-site or off-site change that the project may cause in the environment on cultural heritage or a structure, site or other thing that is of historical or archaeological significance'. Schedule 1 also defines a "site of cultural heritage" as "an antiquity or monument, whether being a place, building, site or structure or a relic, as defined in the Antiquities and Monuments Ordinance". Thus, although the term "cultural heritage" is used, the heritage that is of concern is that as identified as an antiquity or relic in the Antiquities and Monuments Ordinance, or a designated monument.

The EIAO Schedule 2 designates projects requiring HIA by geographic size and location, proximity to known heritage sites and size of the project. Schedule 4 provides that any environmental permit granted may specify timing phasing or mitigation measures to mitigate the impact of a designated project. Mitigation measures include "processes, systems, practices, procedures or technologies for the conservation, preservation or protection of …sites of… cultural heritage importance".

Those undertaking heritage impact assessments are required to engage qualified archaeologists to identify whether there is any possible existence of sites or objects of cultural heritage. This includes underwater projects in the sea around Hong Kong.[7] The Technical Memorandum, Annex 19, provides "Guidelines for assessment of impact on sites of cultural heritage and other impacts". These Guidelines explain that methodologies for assessing impact may vary depending on the site, and that there is "no quantitative standard in deciding the relative importance of these sites, but in general, sites of unique archaeological, historical or architectural value will be considered as highly significant." The Guidelines provide that when undertaking the heritage impact assessment, the following should be included:

1. Baseline Study: to compile a comprehensive inventory of places, buildings, sites and structures of architectural, archaeological and historical value within the proposed project area; and to identify possible threats of destruction in whole or in part of sites of cultural heritage arising from the proposed project.
2. Methodology: information should be assembled to assess the sites to provide detailed geographical, historical, archaeological, ethnographical and other cultural data. Sources for the assessment should include public records, published papers, 'records, archival and historical documents as well as oral legends.'If these sources prove inadequate then field surveys and site investigations shall be conducted to assemble the necessary data.
3. Impact Assessment: the presumption is for 'preservation in totality'. However, if site constraints and other factors permit only partial preservation then 'this must be fully justified with alternative proposals or layout designs which confirm the impracticability of total preservation.' Total destruction is the 'very last resort' and 'shall only be recommended with a meticulous and careful analysis

---

[7] Coroneos [2].

balancing the interest of preserving the archaeological, historical, architectural and other cultural values as against that of the community as a whole.'
4. Mitigation Measures: mitigation measures shall not be used to avoid total or partial preservation.

If archaeological material is discovered, then the Antiquities and Monuments Office must be notified to seek guidance on its significance and the preparation of appropriate mitigation measures.

7.3.3 Revitalizing Historic Buildings Through Partnership Scheme

The Revitalizing Historic Buildings through Partnership Scheme is inspired by Historic England's Constructive Conservation in Practice approach.[8] The fundamental principle of this approach is that the best way to ensure the preservation of old buildings is to find a sustainable new use for them. In Hong Kong the key phrase is "adaptive reuse".[9] This is particularly true for government-owned historic buildings. Therefore, the Scheme is to encourage "constructive conservation" and promote the re-use of historic buildings. The emphasis is on preserving in such way that the building may be used for socially beneficial purposes with as little financial input from the public purse as possible. The Government will usually pay for all initial costs related to renovations of the government-owned heritage buildings, and then rent the buildings to service providers of a social enterprise at a highly subsidized rate. The service provider will not have to reimburse for the initial renovations, but they will have to operate the enterprise using their own funds. What makes this scheme unique is that the service provider is chosen through an application process sent from Non-Profit-making Organizations (NPO) to the Commissioner for Heritage's Office. The historical buildings must be used for the public good and remain open to the public. The stated purposes of the Scheme are[10]:

- "To preserve and put historic buildings into good and innovative use.
- To transform historic buildings into unique cultural landmarks.
- To promote active public participation in the conservation of historic buildings.
- To create job opportunities in particular at the district level."

Bearing in mind the Scheme's stated purposes, the applications are assessed according to four main criteria:

1. how the historical significance of the buildings can be brought out effectively;
2. how the historic buildings would be preserved;

---

[8] Historic England [6].
[9] Conserve and Revitalize Hong Kong Heritage [1].
[10] Conserve and Revitalize Hong Kong Heritage [1].

3. how the community would be benefited, i.e. the social value of the proposal, e.g. jobs created at the district level, benefits to the local community or community at large such as from an educational, cultural, art or medical point of view; and
4. how the social enterprise would operate in terms of financial viability, i.e. the business plan.

The Scheme has now been in operation for almost thirteen years and has some noted successes which we will discuss in the next chapter.

7.3.4 Economic Incentives and Financial Support to Owners of Historic Properties

The Chef Executive also committed to provide economic incentives to encourage private owners of historic properties to conserve them, and to provide financial support to maintain privately owned graded historic buildings. This provision has been used to prevent development of notable examples of built heritage which are in private hands, for example Hung Lau or the "Red House" in Tuen Mun, again discussed in the next chapter.

7.4 Intangible Cultural Heritage Policy

Another product of the social unrest in 2007 is Hong Kong's policy of recognising and celebrating its intangible cultural heritage. The People's Republic of China has embraced the concept of intangible cultural heritage and its protection, being an early member of the Convention for the Safeguarding of the Intangible Cultural Heritage 2003, and expressly including Hong Kong in this membership. Thus, Hong Kong was obliged to conduct a review of its intangible cultural heritage under China's commitments. However, it was surely no coincidence that the Intangible Cultural Heritage Advisory Committee (ICHAC) was set up to guide the survey on Hong Kong's intangible cultural heritage in 2008. Intangible cultural heritage protection is a useful way to gain popular support, as it is usually merely a celebrating and recording of heritage. Thus it requires little expenditure and is thus considerably cheaper than investing in protecting built heritage. It requires little real law to be implemented, if any, and is often seen as a unifying force. It also, usually does not involve claims that anyone's property rights have been infringed.[11]

---

[11] However, there have been and are on-going disputes in their jurisdictions involving issues with intangible cultural heritage and intellectual property rights, cultural appropriation and cultural theft. For example, the dispute between the producers of Prosecco wine in Italy and Prošek wine in Croatia: see Gallagher [5].

7.5 Conclusions on the Government's Heritage Concessions

Although there have been failures in Hong Kong's built heritage protection since 2007, the changes in policy and initiatives implemented after the unrest of 2006 and 2007 have proved quite successful in protecting more of Hong Kong's built heritage. The failures and successes of these changes since 2007 will be discussed in the next chapter.

References

1. Conserve and Revitalize Hong Kong Heritage. Policy statement. https://www.heritage.gov.hk/en/rhbtp/about.htm. Accessed 9 June 2021
2. Coroneos C (2006) The four commandments: the response of Hong Kong SAR to the impact of Seabed development on underwater Cultural Heritage. In: Grenier R, Nutley D, Cochran I (eds) Heritage at Risk Special Edition, Underwater Cultural Heritage at Risk, International Council on Monuments and Sites. ICOMOS, Paris
3. Development Bureau. Replacing Technical Circular (Works) No. 11/2007
4. Donald Tsang, Chief Executive's Policy Address 2007. A New Direction for Hong Kong. pp 49–56. http://www.policyaddress.gov.hk/07-08/eng/policy.html. Accessed 9 June 2021
5. Gallagher SB (2020) Prošek or prosecco: intellectual property or intangible cultural Heritage? In: Chaisse J, Dias Simões F, Friedmann D (eds) Wine law and policy: from national terroirs to a global market. Brill Nijhoff, Leiden
6. Historic England. 7 October 2008. Constructive Conservation in Practice. https://www.historicengland.org.uk/images-books/publications/constructive-conservation-in-practice/. Accessed 9 June 2021
7. South China Morning Post. Lee K. 24 December 2006. Tsang softens stance on heritage conservation. https://www.scmp.com/article/576526/tsang-softens-stance-heritage-conservation. Accessed 9 June 2021
8. Technical Circular (Works) No. 6/2009. Heritage Impact Assessment Mechanism for Capital Works Projects. Antiquities and Monuments Office. Heritage Impact Assessments. http://www.amo.gov.hk/en/hia_02.php. Accessed 9 June 2021

Chapter 8
Hong Kong Built Heritage Failures and Successes Post-2007

Abstract Hong Kong's built heritage protection since 2007 has seen failures and successes. An attempt to nominate the Chi Lin Nunnery as a potential World Heritage Site for China drew criticism and scorn from the public and heritage professionals. The much praised heritage impact policy has seen very public failures, not in the identification of heritage, but in the failure of those who receive assessments to take note of them. There have also been projects acclaimed as successes by some but criticised by others, including the Disney fication of the Marine Police Headquarters Compound as "1881 Heritage". The Urban Renewal Authority has received criticism for the loss of Nga Tsin Wai Tsuen but has been lauded for the Blue House, Wan Chai. There have been further proposed monument declarations with failure and success. The recommendations of a Consultation on Built Heritage Preservation have not been followed, but there have been a number of successful projects under the Revitalizing Historic Buildings through Partnership Scheme, and a notable public–private partnership in Tai Kwun. The Antiquities Advisory Board's Grading System has been criticised as ineffective but has drawn attention to some important built heritage which has been saved, most notably, the State Theatre, North Point.

8.1 Introduction

There have been some notable successes and failures in protecting built heritage in Hong Kong since the changes in government policy post 2007. In particular, it can be noted that there is more consultation and note taken of public opinion in heritage related decisions. For example, the Urban Renewal Authority has committed to more public consultation on its projects, as mandated by statute, although there have still been some unpopular decisions.

The government has declared 46 monuments in the period from 2008 to December 2020 with continued input from the Antiquities Advisory Board and more extensive use of the grading system. The government has also twice used the proposed monument designation to protect buildings from development, one seemingly successful and one noted failure. The latter again spurred public outcry and criticism of Hong

Kong's built heritage policy. In addition, there has been criticism of the implementation of the heritage impact assessments policy. However, there have been notable successes with the Revitalizing Historic Buildings through Partnership Scheme. We will consider some of the failures and successes beginning with the more problematic and moving to the successes.

8.2 Hong Kong Built Heritage Problems and Failures Post-2007

Even after the implementation of amended and innovative polices for built heritage protection in Hong Kong, there have still been some notable failures and embarrassing escapades involving built heritage in Hong Kong since 2007. Most notably the apparent attempt to identify the Chi Lin Nunnery as a World Heritage List contender, and the two publicly recognised failures of the much praised heritage impact assessment scheme.

8.2.1 World Heritage Site: 2012 Victoria Harbour or Chi Lin Nunnery?

China has an incredible range of built heritage and now has as many items inscribed on the World Heritage List as Italy-55 each of the 1,121 designated United Nations Educational, Scientific and Cultural Organization (UNESCO) sites-joint first in the world.[1] The World Heritage List was established under the UNESCO 1972 Convention Concerning the Protection of the World Cultural and Natural Heritage. Hong Kong is a member of the Convention, one of only two international heritage conventions it is party to, the other being the 2003 Convention for the Safeguarding of the Intangible Cultural Heritage, which China specifically joined the Hong Kong SAR to. However, Hong Kong does not have any heritage-natural or cultural—inscribed on the World Heritage List. The nearest World Heritage site to Hong Kong, is the Historic Centre of Macao.[2]

In December 2012 it was reported that Hong Kong Officials had decided to nominate the Chi Lin Nunnery, in Diamond Hill, Kowloon, as a contender for a World Heritage designation for China's "tentative list".[3] This news was greeted with derision by many, as the Nunnery, although aesthetically pleasing, was only completed in 1998 and had only begun to be constructed in 1949. Critical comments included, "It was built in the Tang Dynasty style but not during the Tang Dynasty," and "It

---

[1] World Economic Forum [70]; UNESCO. The World Heritage List [65].
[2] UNESCO World Heritage Sites [64].
[3] South China Morning Post. Ng J. 18 December 2012 [47].

8.2 Hong Kong Built Heritage Problems and Failures Post-2007

was built using wood, which is traditional, but the wood comes from Canada."[4] One member of the Antiquities Advisory Board was particularly vocal in criticism, Tim Ko, historian, noting the nunnery "has nothing to do with the historical development of Hong Kong," At a meeting on 17 December, the Antiquities Advisory Board noted it was not consulted in the matter and expressed shock that it had been bypassed by those seeking to promote the heritage value of the Nunnery.[5]

The other striking factor about the supposed suggestion was the omission to nominate the Victoria Harbour—which is visually synonymous with Hong Kong and represents the reason for the establishment of the British colony and its subsequent success. This was particularly surprising as the Victoria Harbour should easily satisfy the World Heritage Committee in having "outstanding universal value", as it fulfils most if not all of the 10 selection criteria. For example, it is a "masterpiece of human creative genius," exhibiting "an important interchange of human values, over a span of time", and "within a cultural area of the world" as a development "in architecture…technology, monumental arts, town-planning [and] landscape design", containing "superlative natural phenomena" and being "directly or tangibly associated with events or living traditions."[6] The Victoria Harbour was not nominated despite the recommendation that it should be from three independent experts appointed by the government.[7]

At the time, it was suggested that the administration had not nominated the Victoria Harbour because of fears it would no longer be able to develop the land around it. Although this was pointed out as a mistaken understanding of the effect of listing, it seems this was a major concern. Additionally, something not discussed at the time, the government may have been reluctant to have Hong Kong's only World Heritage List contender bearing the name of the British queen under which it became a colony-government administrators tend to refer to the Victoria Harbour as "the Harbour".

There is now some dispute about the veracity of these reports, with referenced sources online being difficult to trace today. However, the fact this become a debate evidences some of the problems with Hong Kong's built heritage protection and the reaction of the public to the story evidences the importance the Hong Kong people give the protection of their heritage, including their colonial heritage.

8.2.2 Heritage Impact Assessment Policy

The policy change effected in 2007, whereby all government capital building projects must have a heritage impact assessment under the Environmental Impact Assessment Ordinance provisions, has been described as the "gold standard" for heritage protection. However, the reality does not fit the perception of these policy as there have also

---

[4] Lai [23].
[5] South China Morning Post. Ng J. 18 December 2012 [47].
[6] UNESCO World Heritage List [63].
[7] South China Morning Post. Franchineau H. 20 January 2013 [34].

been serious failings in the system. This is because heritage impact assessments have been carried out on sites which have subsequently been found to contain archaeologically and/or historically interesting evidence, for example the well at Sacred Hill and the metal remains discovered in the reclamation project of the Victoria Harbour at Wan Chai, which may be HMS Tamar. In the light of these examples it may be questioned whether the assessments missed these possibly important heritage sites or whether those receiving the reports ignored their contents. As more evidence has been released regarding these two notable instances, the latter seems more likely. In fact, in both instances it has been claimed the archaeologists involved informed those they were reporting to that there was a very high likelihood that something of archaeological or historical importance would be affected by the development, and the projects continued unchanged. This raises the more fundamental question- whether the government as commissioner of the assessment about their project should be the decider of whether and how to proceed on the project in the light of the assessment?

8.3 Hong Kong Built Heritage Positives and Successes Post-2007

Although there may be some dispute about what is a positive or success in built heritage preservation, protection and policy, and some of the following examples may be controversial as successes, the author would assert there have been some noted examples of excellent practice in built heritage protection in Hong Kong in recent years and all of following deserve mention as indicating at least some degree of success.

8.3.1 Marine Police Headquarters Compound– "1881 Heritage "or "Disney Heritage"?

Previously, we discussed the Hong Kong Heritage Society's battle in the 1970s to save the Kowloon Canton Railway (KCR) Station and the Marine Police Station in Tsim Sha Tsui from demolition. Although the KCR Station was demolished the Old Marine Police Headquarters was not and in 1994 it was finally declared a monument.[8] However, controversy continued with the building and site when it was developed into "1881 Heritage" between 2005 and 2009. Criticism included the method of preservation and the failure to protect many of what were originally identified as the important heritage elements of the original site, including certain trees.[9] Perhaps most fundamental was that the "hill" on which the Compound stood, the original reasoning for the siting of the Marine Police Headquarters, was largely removed

---

[8] AMO 51.
[9] Dewolf C. Zolimacitymag.com [17]. 26 March 2020.

to allow construction of an upmarket shopping mall. Although the police station and other heritage elements have been retained the development may be considered "Disney Heritage", as it has become a shopping and restaurant centre with a central area reserved for cartoon figures or seasonal displays. Of course, many would support the commercial reuse of the site, arguing that preserving old sites without finding a new use is the main reason that there is opposition to heritage preservation. It may also be argued that shopping is part of Hong Kong's cultural heritage. It should also be noted that the name "1881 Heritage", also criticised by some as Disney fication, is inaccurate as buildings are usually designated by the date of completion in which case this should be "1884 Heritage", but the number four in Cantonese is a homophone for "death" and very unlucky!

Overall the author would suggest it is better to have a Disney fied heritage site which is visited by many than a new development.

8.3.2 Urban Renewal Authority Since 2007

The criticism of the Urban Renewal Authority for not engaging in the Wedding Card Street redevelopment, in spite of its statutory commitment to consult or consider opinion, drew public criticism in 2007. This criticism together with the other subsequent problems has led to more public consultation by the URA. This has seemingly led to more successful projects such as the "Green House Project" in Wan Chai. This is one of the last existing *tong lau* in Hong Kong. The *tong lau* [唐 樓] is usually translated as "Chinese House" as the characters refer to the Tang dynasty in China, a term often used for the Chinese people. However, these are a traditional form of "shophouse" common in many of the former colonial cities in Southeast Asia, combining as the term suggests, retail space on the ground floor with living accommodation above. The Green House project is a block of ten tenement houses on Mallory Street and Burrows Street, which was renovated in 2013. The renovation focusing on adaptive reuse was initially hailed a success. However, even this project has been criticized in its sustainability, as its use as a comic store, although linked to its traditional use, was not financially viable and ceased. The project has now been renamed "7 Mallory Street".[10] Again, it should be noted that the buildings have been sympathetically renovated and are protected-it is just the continued use that is problematic and that is often a problem for old buildings.

There has also been some criticism that, even though the Authority has engaged in public consultations on its more recent projects, it still seems to ignore the public's wishes. This has been noted in one heavily criticised loss of built heritage, Nga Tsin Wai Tsuen, and two on-going projects, the Central Market Building and *Tong Lau*, Central. There has also been one other acclaimed success by the URA, the Blue Houses, also in Wan Chai.

---

[10] Urban Renewal Authority [66].

8.3.2.1 Nga Tsin Wai Tsuen

Nga Tsin Wai Tsuen, "the walled village in front of the yamen",[11] was a walled village near the infamous Kowloon Walled City. It was the last remaining walled village in the urban built-up areas of Hong Kong. The village could trace its history back to 1352 and the founding of its Tin Hau Temple. It was fortified in the early eighteenth century and originally would have had a moat, walls, and watchtowers. However, these were gradually in-filled or removed as the bandits and pirates they were intended to protect against were no longer a threat to the residents.

On 18 July, 2007 the Government and Urban Renewal Authority announced plans to demolish the village and redevelop the site. The Urban Renewal Authority's plan in partnership with Cheung Kong Property Holdings was to replace the village with two high rise tower blocks containing 750 flats plus "some conservation elements". The villagers and heritage activists formed the Nga Tsin Wai Village Concern Group and fought a long campaign to prevent this and protect the village because of its uniqueness and significance in Hong Kong's heritage and historical record. The last residents were forced out of the village in late January 2016 under threat of a fine of up to HK$1 million and imprisonment of six months for not complying with a removal order.

It should be noted that, as the URA has made clear, many residents had moved out or demolished their own properties before the URA began its project, because of the unsanitary conditions. Thus, the redevelopment fitted with the URA's main purpose. Also the URA has committed to preserve some important elements of the village in the new development, as stated on its website[12]:

> The design will adopt an innovative concept of "Conservation by Design" to preserve three relics of the village, namely the village gatehouse, the embedded stone tablet and the Tin Hau Temple, and the central axis linking them up in the walled village setting as the core design elements for the Conservation park to manifest the ambience of the 600 years-old village whilst residential redevelopment could proceed in parallel.

The redevelopment is targeted for completion by 2023/24.

8.3.2.2 Central Market Building

The Central Market Building is the 4th market building on the site which has been used as a market for close on 150 years. The present Bauhaus-style building was built in 1939 and is an example of Functionalism ("form follows function").[13] The revitalisation project has involved years of public consultation but is a subject of great controversy in Hong Kong. In 2003 the government announced plans to redevelop the site. However, the many parties consulted on the redevelopment have failed to

---

[11] The Yamen was the administrative office of the Kowloon Walled City and is preserved in Kowloon Walled City Park.

[12] Urban Renewal Authority. Redevelopment [68].

[13] Urban Renewal Authority. Heritage Preservation & Revitalisation [67].

agree on the buildings future even though shops on the walkway above the market have been shut for a number of years. In 2017 the Urban Renewal Authority was tasked with revitalising the site and preserving its heritage under a HK$740 million plan. But concerns have been expressed that no one knows exactly what the plan is, leading some activist groups such as the Central Market Concern Group to accuse the URA of being non-transparent and conspiratorial.[14]

The URA has identified key elements that define the building's character and architectural style, which include: The Atrium; the external facades facing Jubilee Street and Queen Victoria Street; the grand Staircases; 6 different types of market stall clusters; and, the column grid. The URA targets to complete the project by 2021/22, and it is on-going at the time of writing, June 2021.[15]

8.3.2.3 *Tong Lau*, Central

The *tong lau* in Central are the remains of 10 tenement houses built in 1879 between Cochrane Street and Gutzlaff Street near the Mid-Levels escalator. The area was formerly called City of Victoria. Heritage expert Dr Lee Ho-yin has noted the three-storey houses at the site at the time measured only four metres wide, with over 70 people living in a single block. Built back-to-back, the tenement houses are the city's only surviving remains of that specific construction method from the late nineteenth century. The construction method was discontinued following an outbreak of the plague in 1894, which led to legislation being passed in 1903 forbidding the construction of back-to-back houses with all houses subsequently separated by lanes to ensure proper hygiene and ventilation.[16]

Despite their historical and social significance, the Antiquities Advisory Board decided not to assess the heritage value of the remains for an official grading. After a public campaign to save the remains of the buildings, the Urban Renewal Authority promised in March 2017 to consider an in-situ preservation of the remains of a buildings cluster instead of the original mooted option of dismantling them and reassembling with salvaged bricks on the original site, but in a smaller area.[17]

8.3.2.4 Blue House, Wan Chai

As a notable success for the URA, in 2017 the Blue House cluster was given the Award of Excellence in four categories, in the UNESCO Asia–Pacific Awards for Cultural Heritage Conservation. The cluster is three twentieth century *tong lau* or

---

[14] South China Morning Post. Alex Lo. 22 November 2017 [32].
[15] Central Market [12].
[16] See Antiquities Advisory Board, Historic Building Appraisal N262, December 2016 [1].
[17] South China Morning Post. Ng N. 12 March 2017 [50]; South China Morning Post. Ng N. 13 March 2017 [51].

shop house blocks in Wan Chai, which had once been threatened with demolition. Judges noted the "truly inclusive approach to urban conservation" that had been adopted in converting the buildings into a modern residential and community complex. The project took four years and was overseen by St James' Settlement, a charity, with a government grant of HK$76 million. The historic buildings were turned into a multifunctional complex, which includes 20 residential flats, a community service centre, two restaurants run by social enterprises, and a space dedicated to record and exhibit Hong Kong stories.

This was the first time Hong Kong received the highest level of achievement, which is presented to projects that display exceptional achievement in all criteria and have a "major catalytic impact" at the national or regional level, but 17 other projects in the city have also been given honourable mentions or merit prizes since the awards began in 2000. The judges also noted: "This unprecedented civic effort to protect marginalised local heritage in one of the world's most high-pressure real estate markets is an inspiration for other embattled urban districts in the region and beyond."[18]

8.3.3 Proposed Monument Declarations

The declaration of a proposed monument is an emergency measure to protect a site while deliberations are made about its future. The declaration has only been made six times since it was introduced in 1982. The buildings involved were:

- Ohel Leah Synagogue in 1980. This first declaration seemed to have failed as the declaration was withdrawn and the Synagogue was to be demolished. However, the developers changed their minds, as noted earlier, and the Synagogue was preserved in the development.
- The Morrison Building in 2003. The government negotiated with the owner to preserve the building and provided financial and other support. The Building was declared a monument in 2004.
- Jessville Mansion in 2007. The declaration was withdrawn in February 2008[19] and the mansion is still not a declared monument.[20]
- King Yin Lei in 2007. The government used the declaration to stop the development and negotiated a land swap with the owner for the building. King Yin Lei was declared a monument in 200
- Ho Tung Gardens in 2011. The government negotiated to buy the property or offer a land swap but the owner would not agree and the declaration was withdrawn and Ho Tung Gardens was demolished in 2013, as discussed below.

---

[18] South China Morning Post. Ng N, 1 November, 2017.
[19] See Legislative Council Brief DEVB/CS/CR 4/1/83. February 2008 [24].
[20] See South China Morning Post. 20 November 2012 [31].

- Hung Lau in 2017. The government negotiated with the owner and has provided financial support for preservation work with a guarantee the building will not be developed for 10 years.

The declaration of a proposed monument gives the government time to negotiate with the owner of the built heritage. The government may offer to buy the building, offer a land-swap for the land on which the built heritage is, or offer financial and other support to the private owner of the land if they preserve the built heritage. Although not declared a proposed monument, as the owners agreed to wait and negotiate with the government, Kom Tong Hall, purchased by the government for $53 million in 2002, is an example of the government purchasing an important building facing redevelopment. Land-swap was arranged for King Yin Lei and it became the government's property and a monument.[21] The government may also use land swap to protect other land that is of value to Hong Kong, for example land that is ecologically important, as in the landfill and industrial land swapped with a private developer to build a golf course in return for most of Tai Po's Sha Lo Tung.[22] Financial and other support was provided to the owners of the Morrison Building and Hung Lau. The Morrison Building is now a monument. Hung Lau is subject to an agreement it will not be demolished for a ten-year period from the provision of the financial support and negotiation is ongoing for further protection.

Arguably the declaration of these six proposed monuments has been successful, as two were later declared monuments, two have been protected by negotiation with their owners, thus their proposed monument declarations were withdrawn. Jessville Mansion has not been declared a monument but has also not been developed. Only one has been demolished, Ho Tung Gardens. The fact that four of these declarations have been made since the 2006–7 protests evidence the government adopting a more attentive attitude to public heritage concern. Even in the case of Ho Tung gardens, the government arguably tried as hard as was practicable to come to a negotiated settlement with the private owner.

8.3.3.1 Ho Tung Gardens

Ho Tung Gardens was a villa built on the Peak by the prominent local Chinese Sir Robert Ho Tung Bosman.[23] It was exceptional in that it was the earliest building built by a Eurasian on the Peak. This was because the Peak had been subject to restrictions on occupation by Chinese. The Peak District Reservation Ordinance 1904 restricted occupation of the Peak to non-Chinese and made it an offence subject to injunction by the Supreme Court for "any owner, lessee, tenant, or occupier of any land or building within the Peak District to let such land or building or any part thereof for

---

[21] Yeung [71].
[22] South China Morning Post. Kao. E. 15 June, 2017 [42].
[23] 22 December 1862—26 April 1956.

the purpose of residence by any but non-Chinese, or to permit any but non-Chinese to reside on or in such land or building".[24]

The draconian provisions of the Ordinance were relaxed for the benefit of the non-Chinese in that Section 5 provided that it did, "not apply to servants of the residents in the Peak District living on the premises of their, employers, to licensed chair coolies -and jinrikisha [rickshaw] coolies plying for hire in such district, to contractors or labourers temporarily residing and actually employed in such district, to inmates of hotels or hospitals in such district, or to visitors at the house of any resident in the said district."

The Ordinance was repealed in 1930.

Sir Robert Ho Tung was given permission by the Governor in Council, under the exemption provision in Section 4 of the Ordinance,[25] to build a garden and house on the Peak because of his exceptional service to the British in Hong Kong and China. In 1927 he had helped mediate a strike that had caused much disruption in Canton (Guangzhou) and Hong Kong.[26] The strike was in retaliation for British Sikh police opening fire on Chinese in Shanghai with at least nine killed and many wounded. The Kuomintang circulated pamphlets which called for Chinese to rise up against the British. Many Chinese left the colony and there were food shortages and fears of poisoned water supplies. The strike threatened the very existence of Hong Kong as the British government had to make a large loan to the colony to keep it going-something that is always beyond the pale. Although granted the exemption as thanks for his actions under Section 4 of the Ordinance, it should also be noted that Robert Ho Tung was Eurasian with a Dutch father and Chinese mother.

In 2009, Ho Tung Gardens was identified as a Grade I historic building by the Antiquities Advisory Board. Bernard Chan, Chairman of the AAB noted that:

> The choice of a very Chinese-looking style of architecture for the new house in 1927 ... was a statement that a racial barrier was being broken. It was also a declaration by Hotung that he was different from his neighbours, who were only living in the colony temporarily before going home.

The owner of the premises, Ho Min-kwan, Sir Robert Ho Tung's granddaughter, objected to the Grade I rating on the grounds that Ho Tung had never lived in the property, there were no important family events held there, and the building's interior had been considerably altered over the years.[27] At the end of 2010, Ms Ho applied for a building permit to demolish the mansion and build 11 blocks of four-storey houses on the site. The development plan was estimated to be worth HK$3 billion at the then-market price. The Building Department had no authority to do other than consider the plan's structural issues and so issued an approval in December 2010, but

---

[24] The Peak District Reservation Ordinance 1904, Sections 3 & 6. Available via Historical Laws of Hong Kong Online [18].

[25] Soong Mei-ling (Madam Chiang Kai-shek) was similarly granted exemption to reside on the Peak: see Wordie [69], pp. 74–75.

[26] The Canton- Hong Kong Strike June 1925 to October 1926.

[27] South China Morning Post. Ng. J. 26 January 2011 [38].

did alert the Antiquities and Monuments Office.[28] Government officials attempted to negotiate with the owner but received little cooperation and so, on 28 January 2011, for only the fourth time in its history, the Antiquities and Monuments Ordinance was used by the Government to declare Ho Tung Gardens a proposed monument. The Government negotiated with the owner about purchasing the property and suggested a land swap. However, she was adamant that if she could not demolish and redevelop the site for herself, retaining one of the ten units she intended to build, she would require a huge amount in compensation, approximately HK$7billion- the top end of any valuation. In defence of her plans to demolish her grandfather's house Ho Min-kwan claimed that the existing main building is "unexceptional ... does not have the requisite historical or architectural value or authenticity; it is not a rare example of an architectural style, and it is not a distinctive building structure." Ho also reiterated her claim that her grandfather had never lived there. She also noted that the main building had already been converted into 6 apartments.

Negotiations broke down. The Chief Executive elections were about to take place and the then Chief Executive, Donald Tsang was about to be replaced, and seemed inclined to leave this difficult decision to his successor. In December 2012 the government, under the new Chef Executive, Leung Chun-ying, announced that it would not declare the site a monument and so the protection would lapse. The decision was justified on the grounds that compensation payable to the owner would be huge and disproportionate to the benefit to Hong Kong.[29]

Demolition work began in July 2013 and was completed in October. The Secretary for Development, Paul Chan, admitted there had been a policy failure but noted the truth in the Government's claim that, "not everyone would agree with spending billions of dollars of public money on private heritage sites". In January 2015 the site was sold for HK5.1Billion, $2 billion less than Ho Min-kwan had asked the Government. The buyer was understood to be the mainland tycoon Cheung Chung-kiu who has been dubbed the "Li Ka-shing of Chongqing". It was also speculated that the buyer could save $1 billion in tax breaks and so receive the property for $3billion less than the Government had been asked to pay. The new AAB chairman Andrew Lam Siu-lo commented: "Although we failed to save the house, I still hope the developer will conserve the garden in an innovative way to reflect the history of the complex...The transacted price is a market price...It will be a good reference for public discussion under a public consultation on heritage conservation. Are we willing to pay for it?".

Arguably, the government's decision not to use such an amount of public funds for what was a significant historical but not an historic building was justified. Particularly as the government had, as part of the fallout of the tumultuous year of 2007, land swapped for Ho Tung's younger brother's house, King Yin Lei, which remains empty and unused today.

---

[28] South China Morning Post. Ng. J. 26 January 2011 [39].

[29] For a full discussion of the issue of compensation in this case with regard to the Antiquities and Monuments Ordinance see Chen [13].

8.3.3.2 Hung Lau ("Red House"), Tuen Mun

The Red House in Tuen Mun was built between 1905 and 1910 and is widely believed to have served as a secret base for the Revolution of 1911 in China led by Sun Yat-sen. The land the Red House sits on includes a park named after Dr Sun Yat Sen where groups affiliated with Taiwan, where Sun is revered as the "father of the nation", gather to celebrate the anniversary of the 1911 Revolution, on October 10, every year. The present landlord bought the house for HK$5 million in November, 2016. The Antiquities and Monuments Office (AMO) classified the Red House a grade one historic building in 2009, mainly for its "factor of collective memory". Although this is the highest grading, meaning it is a building of "outstanding merit, which every effort should be made to preserve if possible", this does not give it statutory protection. When it was noted that the private owner was trying to evict residents, had cut off their water supply and had begun to tear down the building there was a public outcry. Members of the public called for the building to be declared a monument to protect it because of its historical value to Hong Kong and China. However, at a special meeting in February, 2017, the Antiquities Advisory Board considered it unnecessary to trigger a proposed monument declaration at that moment as there was no imminent demolition threat and the government had been in talks with the owner on preservation proposals.[30] But at the meeting, board chairman Andrew Lam Siu-lo stressed that he would not hesitate to trigger the mechanism necessary to make the declaration "right away" should the building be further damaged. The decision, he said, could be made within days.

Although the government initially thought it had achieved a negotiated delay in the development to permit discussions about its future, workers were filmed tearing out windows. Building Department Officials issued an order to the owner to stop the work noting that any alterations or demolition required government approval.[31] In March 2017 the government declared the building a proposed monument to prevent further damage, while seeking further discussions with the owner about how to better conserve it.

In October, 2017, it seemed the Red House would be saved for at least 10 years when the owner applied to the government under a subsidy scheme to restore historic buildings.[32] In a paper submitted to the Legislative Council, the Development Bureau said there would be a condition that the owner could not demolish the Red House or transfer ownership for 10 years from the completion of the maintenance works.

---

[30] South China Morning Post. Ng K, Ng N. 17 February, 2017 [48].
[31] South China Morning Post. Kao E. 9 March, 2017 [41].
[32] South China Morning Post. Zhao S. 26 October, 2017 [60].

8.3.4 Consultation on Built Heritage Preservation

One positive that came from the failure to protect Ho Tung Gardens was the Consultation on Built Heritage Preservation. In his 2013 Policy Address, after the public debates and criticism of the failure to prevent the demolition of Ho Tung Gardens, the Chief Executive, Leung Chun-ying, noted the challenges for the conservation of built heritage, in particular for privately-owned historic buildings[33]:

> We have worked to strike a balance between the need to respect private property rights and the need to preserve our heritage. On the premise of respecting private property rights, we need to offer appropriate economic incentives to encourage private owners to either hand over or conserve historic buildings in their ownership. In light of the experience gained over the past few years, we need to review the policy on the conservation of privately-owned historic buildings. This will include formulating a set of more detailed mechanism and criteria for determining the extent and means to use public resources for the conservation of privately-owned historic buildings, and studying whether there is a need to enhance conservation of such buildings in the context of town planning.

The Antiquities Advisory Board was invited by the Development Bureau to take part in this review. The Consultation was entitled "Respecting our Heritage While Looking Ahead: Policy on Conservation of Built Heritage Consultation Paper". The Paper's introduction noted the importance of built heritage and the problems with its conservation[34]:

"Preservation of historic buildings will undoubtedly be beneficial to society. However, preservation costs and public resources will always be involved no matter whether the historic buildings are privately or government-owned and can be very substantial. High maintenance costs for historic buildings, coupled with the high land costs in Hong Kong, mean that the Government may have to offer significant amounts of compensation to owners for their loss of development rights arising from the preservation of historic buildings…

The AAB wishes to know the views of the public on the following major issues: how to enhance protection for historic buildings while giving due regard to private property rights and development needs, how to share the cost of conservation, and the amount of resources the community is prepared to invest in conservation work."

The consequent Report gave Recommendations falling into three areas:

(I) Setting up a built heritage fund: public education and publicity activities, academic researches, public engagement and consultation programmes. It should also cover certain government initiatives and activities on built heritage conservation
(II) Providing additional incentives and facilitation
(III) The next step: examine setting up of statutory grading system in the longer run for protection of graded buildings while safeguarding private property rights application of "point-line-plane" concept, the Administration should

---
[33] Conserve and Revitalise Hong Kong Heritage [15].
[34] Antiquities Advisory Board [5].

as first step conduct study to explore feasibility of conserving and protecting selected building cluster(s) of unique heritage value under the "point-line-plane" approach

In medium term, arrange thematic surveys or mapping exercises on building cluster(s) of heritage value for drawing up appropriate conservation strategies and protection measures if necessary, and for future planning

The author considered including the Consultation on Built Heritage Preservation in the first part of this chapter as a failure, as, to date, the Recommendations have not been followed. However, the fact there was a consultation and that it is there as guidance of future policy development should be viewed as a positive, along with the successes detailed in this part.

8.3.5 Revitalizing Historic Buildings Through Partnership Scheme

The Scheme has been well-received in Hong Kong although there has been some criticism. As noted in the previous chapter, to fulfil the Scheme's stated purposes, the applications are assessed according to four main criteria:

1. how the historical significance of the buildings can be brought out effectively;
2. how the historic buildings would be preserved;
3. how the community would be benefited, i.e. the social value of the proposal, e.g. jobs created at the district level, benefits to the local community or community at large such as from an educational, cultural, art or medical point of view; and
4. how the social enterprise would operate in terms of financial viability, i.e. the business plan.

Examples of successes of the scheme include the Old Tai O Police Station, which was one of the first projects, and the Blue House as discussed above. Although officially not part of the Scheme, the government and the Hong Kong Jockey Club worked in partnership for the successful conservation of the central Police Station, Tai Kwun.

8.3.5.1 Old Tai O Police Station

Built in 1902 and identified as a Grade II historical building by the AAB. After reviewing all the applications, Hong Kong Heritage Conservation Foundation Ltd (HCF), was selected to revitalize the Old Tai O Police Station into a heritage themed boutique hotel.[35] The Tai O Heritage Hotel opened in 2012, with the stated purpose of allowing visitors, tourists, and the Tai O community to establish a closer connection

---

[35] Conserve and Revitalise Hong Kong Heritage [15].

with the historic site.³⁶ To meet the first two criteria of the scheme, HCF reinstated the two-story main block, the outhouse extension, the bunkers, the cannons, and the guard towers, to their original appearances. The front façade was not to be disturbed by the alterations and the new required parts of the hotel have been created on the back elevation. Following conservation guidelines, all such works are reversible. The boutique hotel has nine suites, a rooftop restaurant called the Tai O Lookout, which serves dishes made with Tai O's own ingredients, and a heritage interpretation room converted from the old reporting room and prison cell. To meet the third criterion, the Heritage Interpretation Room conducts a free heritage guided tour daily and there are books, maps and video documentaries on Tai O and Old Tai O Police Station available. The Hotel operates as a non-profit social enterprise, with all surpluses being used for conservation and maintenance of historic buildings, to promote and protect the cultural heritage of Tai O and its natural environment, and to promote the local economy and tourism. Although the capital cost for the project was HK$69.13 million, no financial support from the government has been required since, which fulfils the fourth criterion.

8.3.5.2 Tai Kwun-Central Police Station

The Central Police Station Complex was built between 1864 and 1925. The complex, colloquially known as Tai Kwun or Big Station, a declared monument, consists of three main groups of buildings, including the police station, the former Central Magistracy and Victoria Prison. The prison, first built in the 1840s and reconstructed in the 1860s, only ceased to function in 2006, making it Hong Kong's longest operating prison. The Compound has been an important part of Hong Kong's heritage, as it has been involved in notable historic events. For example, Vietnamese revolutionary Ho Chi Minh was jailed there for more than six months in 1931, the Japanese military tortured prisoners in the compound during the second world war, and during the bloody 1967 communist riots, officers set up a control room in the compound.³⁷ A project to renovate the complex was first announced in 2007. The HK$1.8 billion revitalization project began in 2011 under the Jockey Club supervision and Antiquities Advisory Board oversight. However, heritage projects do not always progress smoothly. In May 2016 the Jockey Club announced that a wall and part of the roof at the former Married Inspectors' Quarters, one of the 16 historic buildings in the 150-year-old compound, collapsed during renovation work. Although the Jockey Club committed to rebuilding the structures they admitted that such a collapse would inevitably lead to loss of heritage value, delay and overrun costs. In March 2018 it was announced that part of the site would open in May 2018, as a heritage and arts centre, after seven years of work.³⁸ However not all were pleased at the opening of the new heritage site as politicians and locals warned of the impact of more visitors to an

---

³⁶ Tai O Heritage Hotel website [62].
³⁷ South China Morning Post. Zhao S. 1 April, 2018.
³⁸ South China Morning Post. Zhao S. 25 March, 2018.

already overcrowded area of Hong Kong and complained of the already inadequate infrastructure with crowded roads and walkways including the mid-levels escalator.[39] Noting these criticisms and some criticism regarding authenticity in renovation, the project is generally considered a success. In 2019, Tai Kwun received the Award of Excellence in the UNESCO Asia–Pacific Awards for Cultural Heritage Conservation, recognising the project's revitalisation efforts.[40] Overall this project must be considered one of the great successes in the recent the history of heritage preservation and protection in Hong Kong.

8.3.5.3 Old Tai Po Police Station

In 2016 the Old Tai Po Police Station, which had been the subject of a five-year-long architectural and environmental revitalization project won an honourable mention in UNESCO's Asia–Pacific Awards for Cultural Heritage Conservation for its transformation into a Green Hub for Sustainable Living and for successfully conserving "a very significant colonial building". The project was part of the government's Revitalising Historic Buildings through Partnership Scheme in 2010 and was overseen by Kadoorie Farm and Botanic Garden. The project cost some HK$50 million.[41]

8.3.6 Declared Monuments

There has also been a noted increase in the rate of gazetting of monuments in this period. Under the colonial government there was a slow start to declaration of monuments with 22 monuments declared between the implementation of the Ordinance and 1983. The negotiations for the Joint Declaration and the realisation that Hong Kong would be returned to China in 1997 did not result in an immediate increase in the number of declared monuments but there was a flurry in the early 1990s. Between 1984 and 1997 there were 41 declarations of monuments. Thus, under the colonial government there was a total of 64 monuments declared.

There are now 126 declared monuments, thus 62 monuments have been declared between 1997 and 2021. The post-colonial government began declaring monuments in a cautious manner with only 17 declarations between 1997 and 2007. Thus, since the issues in 2006 and 2007 there have been a further 45 declarations. This should be viewed as, at least in part, a positive reaction to the public protests.

The monuments declared during the last 14 years cover a variety of buildings and sites, including a number of buildings built during the colonial period linked to followers of Sun Yat Sen, for example the Residence of Ip Ting-sz at Lin Ma Hang Tsuen, Sha Tau Kok, built in 1908 and declared a monument in 2009. Some

---

[39] South China Morning Post, Zhao S. 25 March, 2018.
[40] Conserving Heritage—The Revitalisation of Tai Kwun [16].
[41] South China Morning Post, Singh H. 10 September, 2016.

8.3 Hong Kong Built Heritage Positives and Successes Post-2007

are distinctly colonial in nature and association. For example, King's College in Bonham Road, Mid-Levels, declared a monument in 2011, The Cenotaph, Central, erected in 1923 to commemorate the dead of the First World War and declared a monument in 2013, and military buildings such as the old Lei Yue Mun Barracks, Chai Wan, built in 1895 and declared monuments in 2016. Thus, the post-colonial administration has not shied away from declaring colonial buildings as monuments, and has, at least since the beginning of 2008, declared some difficult built heritage as monuments. In particular, the Cenotaph commemorates some difficult but important times in Hong Kong's history, especially as the Antiquities and Monuments Office website notes that[42]:

> In the 1980s, eight Chinese characters, '英魂不朽 浩氣長存', meaning 'May their martyred souls be immortal, and their noble spirits endure', were carved on one side of the Cenotaph to match the inscription 'The Glorious Dead' and make it clear that the monument commemorates all who died in the wars, especially those who fell in the defence of Hong Kong.

The input of the Antiquities Advisory Board and more extensive use of the grading system has also been a noted feature of some built heritage success and some problems.

8.3.7 The Antiquities Advisory Board Grading System

The Antiquities Advisory Board introduced a grading system for historical buildings in Hong Kong in 1996 to aid the Antiquities and Monuments Office's territory-wide survey of historic buildings which was completed in 200. The grading system was also used in the 2002–2004 more detailed survey. Post 2007, the grading system has become more widely appreciated and also criticised. In 2009 the Grades were defined as[43]:

- Grade I–Building of outstanding merit for which every effort should be made to preserve if possible;
- Grade II–Building of special merit; which efforts should be made to selectively preserve; and
- Grade III–Buildings of some merit, but not yet qualified for consolidation as possible monuments. These buildings are to be recorded and used as a pool from which future monuments may be selected.

---

[42] AMO 102.

[43] [28] publication of the assessment of 1,444 historic buildings.

Grade III or 3 is now usually defined as "Buildings of some merit; preservation in some form would be desirable and alternative means should be considered if preservation is not practicable."[44]

The main criticism of the grading system is that it is purely advisory.[45] If a building is graded at the highest grade, it is still not protected. The grading system is merely to aid the Antiquities and Monuments Office and ultimately the Authority in making decisions about protection to be afforded by declaring proposed monuments and monuments. Therefore, the grading has no legal effect and affords no legal protection to the identified built heritage. Thus, the owner of a graded property may do as they wish with it as long as they contravene no building law or cause a nuisance. Indeed, it may be that grading of a building alerts an owner to possible monument declaration and so encourages deliberate development or accidental demolition.

In March 2009, the Board announced the completion of the assessment of 1,444 historic buildings in Hong Kong. Since then the Board has continued grading other buildings in Hong Kong with reference to information from the Antiquities and Monuments Office and suggestions from the public. Up to 11 March 202, some 1013 historic buildings have been assessed with Grade 1, Grade 2 or Grade 3 status including[46]:

(a)   173 buildings with Grade 1 status;
(b)   338 buildings with Grade 2 status; and
(c)   502 buildings with Grade 3 status.

The website of the Board contains a set of criteria for grading and specimen marking papers in its frequently asked questions.[47] The criteria include:

(a)   historic interest, such as its association with historical event(s), phase(s), activity(ies) and historic figure(s), importance in the historical development of Hong Kong, and/or age of the building
(b)   group value, such as its importance in a building cluster showing common cultural value(s) or historical development of Hong Kong
(c)   architectural merit, such as the contribution of the building's external appearance to visual quality of its vicinity
(d)   authenticity, such as any alterations to the historic building that adversely affect or enhance its heritage or cultural significance and/or architectural value
(e)   social value and local interest, such as its importance in depicting the "cultural identity" and perpetuating the "collective memory" of the community, and

---

[44] See Antiquities Advisory Board. 1,444 Historic Buildings and New Items in addition to 1,444 Historic Buildings—Definition of the Gradings; Antiquities and Monuments Office. Assessment of 1,444 Historic Buildings [3].

[45] See, for example, Kong [22].

[46] Antiquities Advisory Board. 1,444 Historic Buildings and New Items in addition to 1,444 Historic Buildings—Results of the Assessment of 1,444 Historic Buildings [4].

[47] Antiquities Advisory Board. Frequently Asked Questions on Assessment of Buildings in Hong Kong which May Have Heritage Value [6].

8.3 Hong Kong Built Heritage Positives and Successes Post-2007

(f) rarity—being rare due to its historical interest, architectural merit, group value, social value and local interest, and/or authenticity of the building

Thus, buildings have been graded because of their important place in the life of Hong Kong, because of their function and design, but also because of their historical and/or social value, including celebration in local film or literature. For example, Yau Ma Tei police station, built in 1922, has been used in numerous TV dramas and crime movies including *Lee Rock* (1991), *Election* (2005) and *Rush Hour 2* (2001). Thus it has become an iconic building for many. The station was classified as a Grade II historic building in 2009.[48] Many were sad at its closure to the public in 2016 as part of a redevelopment project, although part of the original building, the Old Block, will be preserved.[49]

Since its founding there have been claims of incompetence and corruption made against the Board—in particular there have been high-profile public changes of mind and consequent changes of grading and advice. It has also been accused of misleading the government.[50] After the controversy surrounding Queen's Pier in 2007, the Board made the decision to open its meetings to the public and post minutes of its meetings online to aid in transparency.

More recently, it has been claimed that the grading system has a strategic weakness. The Board consistently identifies post-war architecture as "functional" and thus less deserving of protection than other earlier buildings which may have more apparent, and to some gaudy, architecture and decoration. For example the description "functional" was used in grading decisions regarding the Shaw Studio compound, the State Theatre in North Point and the headquarters of the Garden Company in Sham Shui Po. For the last mentioned, the designation of this building as Grade II, which means it is of "special merit" and should be "selectively" preserved, has been noted by Professor Ho Puay-peng, head of the Department of Architecture in the National University of Singapore and a former member of Hong Kong's Antiquities Advisory Board, as assuring that "the modernist landmark is now set to meet the wrecking ball."[51]

Paul Chan has been a critic of the failure of the Antiquities Advisory Board's grading system to protect Hong Kong's post war built heritage.[52] In particular, he queried the qualification and suitability of those actually making the decisions. Chan noted that the exercise of grading follows a "scoring exercise" in which a five-member assessment panel under the Antiquities Advisory Board, which includes the executive secretary of the Antiquities and Monuments Office (AMO), "scores" the buildings it reviews before proposing grades for the board to adopt, or otherwise. The four members apart from the executive secretary of the Antiquities and Monuments Office were appointed in 2005. The members are officially described as comprising experts in history, architecture, town planning and engineering; however, Chan noted

---

[48] South China Morning Post. Leung C. 31 January, 2017 [44].
[49] Hong Kong Police. Offbeat Online [20]. Yau Ma Tei Police Station.
[50] See for example, Meacham [28].
[51] South China Morning Post. Ho P. 28 March, 2018 [37].
[52] South China Morning Post, 06 April, 2018.

that some of the panel's judgments have been found desperately wanting in recent years. Using the example of the North Point Sate Theatre, Chan noted that some panel members ranked buildings simply by age, ignoring the "importance of their social value or the collective memory they embody." Chan described the official assessment mechanism and criteria for historic buildings in Hong Kong as "both outdated and at odds with public expectations." Chan called for the Development Bureau to undertake an immediate reform of the historic buildings grading system to ensure it was informed by the "broadest, best-informed and most professional input from the community".

Three of the sites which have attracted the most public debate regarding grading decisions in recent years have been the Shaw Studios, the Empire Theatre (State Theatre), North Point, and the Castle Peak Dragon Kiln.

8.3.7.1 Shaw Studios

The Shaw Studios site has been the subject of much controversy. Members of the Antiquities Advisory Board disagreed on the protection to be afforded the buildings comprising the site. Originally in March 2014 the Board agreed that the entire 7.8 ha site should be accorded a grade one listing—the highest possible grading—in recognition of its historic importance for the film industry. Later an assessment panel was tasked to provide individual grading for the 23 buildings. In June, this resulted in only old Shaw House, constructed in 1960, being graded as grade one out of the 23 buildings on the site, with 17 other buildings recommended for lower grades and five not being accorded any grade.[53] Members disagreed with some arguing that the buildings were not very old and should not be afforded the same grading as older buildings in Hong Kong.[54]

In 2018 the developers provided amended development plans for their residential complex. These committed to preserve the grade one Shaw Administration Building and convert it into a commercial facility with gallery/heritage display area. The developers further committed to conserve the Film Store and Dubbing room in this area. In addition, three dormitory blocks, and the Guard House, will be conserved and selected facades/features from Sound Stage 1, Colour Laboratory, Production Department and Shaw Villa will be conserved.[55]

8.3.7.2 Empire Theatre (State Theatre), North Point

In 2017 conservationists raised the issue of the future of the Empire Theatre in North Point. The 1,400-seat theatre complex was opened on 11 December 1952 and

---

[53] South China Morning Post. Fung F. 4 June 2015 [35].

[54] South China Morning Post. Fung F. 05 June, 2015 [36].

[55] Broad Development Parameters of the Applied Use /Development in respect of Application No. A/SK-CWBN/48 [11].

8.3 Hong Kong Built Heritage Positives and Successes Post-2007

changed its name to the State Theatre in 1959. Currently used as a snooker parlour, the Theatre Complex is one of the last post-war stand-alone theatre structures in the city and the only building with an iconic flying buttress. The AAB noted that the building is now the oldest international-class theatre existing in Hong Kong, as well as being the third oldest of all Hong Kong's theatre buildings.[56] The building was originally designated a grade 3 status but news of an on-going attempt to purchase the building for demolition and development in 2015 had prompted activists to call for the Antiquities Advisory Board to upgrade the complex to Category 1. In December 2016 it was designated grade 1. After members of the Antiquities Advisory Board visited the site, they noted that the interior of the theatre was well preserved with original staircases, toilets, and other structures. They also stated that the theatre was part of the collective memory of Hongkongers and deserved to be awarded the top protection grading for historic buildings.[57]

The acquisition of the building had been delayed because of the many different property rights owners in the building complex- there were approximately 450 property rights in the building complex—50 for the theatre, 181 for the shops and 219 for the flats atop the theatre.[58]

In November 2018, New World Development applied for a compulsory sale order for the building. This would allow them to buy out all those with interests in the building and consolidate ownership to apply for permission to develop the site. A spokesman said that while it was "premature" to discuss any future development plan, the group would "actively consider how to preserve the essence of the former State Theatre" after it had successfully unified the ownership.[59]

In January 2019, the Legislative Council's development panel reported that they had agreed with New World Development to preserve the Theatre in any development.[60]

In August 2020 it was reported that New World Development had won its case to compulsorily buy out the owners of the Theatre and would retain the Theatre in the development.[61] To show their commitment to the conservation of the theatre and their appreciation of its heritage importance, the new owners organised tours of the Theatre in April 2021 to permit those interested to see the interior and even visit the iconic concrete arches on the roof.[62] It should be noted that New World Development's CEO and executive vice-chairman. Adrian Cheng Chi-kong, is also the founder of Hong Kong's first art shopping mall, K11 in Tsim Tsha Tsui and expresses his, and his companies' commitment to the arts and heritage.[63] Therefore, things look bright for a sustainable future for the once threatened Sate Theatre.

---

[56] See Antiquities Advisory Board, Historic Building Appraisal N46 [2].

[57] South China Morning Post. Leung S. 8 December 2016 [45].

[58] South China Morning Post. Xinqi S. 11 December, 2017 [54].

[59] South China Morning Post. Cheung E. 22 October 2018.

[60] South China Morning Post. Vetter D. 2 February 2019 [53].

[61] South China Morning Post. Li S. 25 August 2020 [46].

[62] South China Morning Post. Lam N. South China Morning Post. 1 April 2021.

[63] K11. About the Chairman [21].

8.3.7.3 Castle Peak Dragon Kiln

In 2018 Hong Kong residents began a petition to preserve Hong Kong's only complete "dragon kiln".[64] These kilns were tunnel-like pottery ovens which were usually built in the mountains. The last surviving example is at Castle Peak, Tuen Mun and its site is part of an area the government has been trying to rezone as residential and develop for public housing. The Kiln was built in the 1940s by the Castle Peak Pottery Company, which produced ceramic tiles, bricks, wine bottles for the Wing Lee Wai wine factory, and cooking utensils. It has an interesting place in Hong Kong's labour history, as when the Company ceased production it was run by its workers under the name Tao Sing, and Kung Hop Pottery Kiln, or, in English, Workers Co-op Pottery Kiln Commercial production at the kiln had ceased by the 1970s, and artistic production finished in 1982. Thus although not very old its uniqueness and its importance as evidence of the social and economic heritage of Hong Kong has been recognised by Category III grading in 2014.[65] Unfortunately about one-fifth of the kiln site recognised by the Antiquities Advisory Board is not regarded as part of the kiln in the maps produced by the Planning Department.

8.4 Private Built Heritage Protection and Public Private Partnerships

We have already considered a number of public and private partnerships which have been successful in protecting Hong Kong's built heritage, for example under the Revitalising Historic Buildings through Partnership Scheme, such as the Old Tai Po Police Station, and other partnerships, for example the former Police Headquarters in Central- Tai Kwun.

Many individuals, including living individuals, families, and public and private corporations have also used their own funds to purchase and protect built heritage. One noted corporate success is the Old Bank of China Building in Central. This was built in 1951 with its pair of lions on guard at its front doors, right next to the HSBC headquarters, and served as the major office of the Bank of China Hong Kong until 1990, when the 70-floor new Bank of China Tower was completed. Bank of China renovated the old building over a year to celebrate its 150th anniversary in 2017, with the renovated building now forming the headquarters for its BOC Hong Kong private bank.[66]

Of course sometimes these individuals make mistakes. For example, in 2017 an arch above an entrance to the Ruttonjee Hospital, originally called the Seaman's Hospital, in Wan Chai, built in the late 1880s was taken down to make way for a new barrier-free access. The demolition of the arch drew criticism from the public and

---

[64] South China Morning Post. Xinqi S. South China Morning Post, 7 March, 2018.

[65] Hong Kong Free Press. Sala I. 6 March, 2018 [19].

[66] South China Morning Post. Yiu E., 29 August, 2017.

8.4 Private Built Heritage Protection and Public Private Partnerships

media and was condemned by district councillors who had approved the renovation project. Councillors said the Hospital had not told them the project would involve demolishing the arch. The Hospital said it had stored the pieces of the arch and would reassemble it later. The arch was the only remnant of the original Seaman's Hospital but was not subject to any protection order.[67]

As previously noted, a number of clans in the New Territories have protected their clan property, preserved it and made it open to the people of Hong Kong to celebrate the cultural heritage of the clan and the region. Often this has been in partnership with the government in the form of financial assistance. For example, the Tang Clan has established the Ping Shan Trail[68] and the Lung Yuk Tau Trail with the help of the government.[69]

Similarly, individuals and groups have established charitable bodies, sometimes in association with the government, which have protected built heritage.[70] Other notable conservations have included the Tung Wah Coffin Home conserved by a local voluntary association, the Tung Wah Group of Hospitals, in 2005 with the assistance of two heritage conservation awards, one conferred by the Antiquities and Monuments Office (AMO) of the Hong Kong Government, and the other one by the United Nations Educational, Scientific and Cultural Organization (UNESCO).[71]

Sometimes these groups have not found their heritage protection plans unopposed. For example, in 2017 a row erupted between indigenous villagers and those promoting the conservation of the 400-year-old village of Lai Chi Wo in the northern New Territories. The Hong Kong Countryside Foundation, a charity dedicated to conserving the city's countryside, was overseeing the HK$50 million project, funded by the Hong Kong Jockey Club, aimed at revitalizing the area and promoting Hakka culture. The row originated over plans to convert empty dwellings into guest houses, with some villagers who have moved overseas complaining they were not properly consulted and would complain to town planners and even block roads into the village if the project was not shelved. The plan was approved by the Town Planning Board in August 2017 as part of a larger government scheme, the Chief Executive's Community Project, to conserve and promote sustainable development in rural areas.[72] In 2019 the Hong Kong Countryside Foundation Conservation received government approval for the Lai Chi Wo expansion.[73] The Foundation proposed a 20-year lease on 14 houses which would be turned into guest rooms for at most 56 visitors, highlighting Hakka-style heritage. The house owners would then resume privately using their homes when the leases expired. The approval of the scheme in the face of

---

[67] South China Morning Post. Zhao S. 8 March, 2017 [61].

[68] Antiquities and Monuments Office. Heritage Trails. Ping Shan Trail [10].

[69] Antiquities and Monuments Office. Heritage Trails. Lung Yeuk Tau Heritage Trail [9].

[70] For example, the Lord Wilson Heritage Trust, a statutory charitable trust, was established to support heritage projects in Hong Kong under the Lord Wilson Heritage Trust Ordinance (cap. 425) in 1992: see Lord Wilson Heritage Trust website [25].

[71] Ma [26].

[72] South China Morning Post. Kao E, Ng N. 7 November, 2017 [40].

[73] South China Morning Post. Xinqi S. South China Morning Post. 1 February 2019 [30].

Fig. 8.1 Heritage 1881

opposition from the indigenous villagers may reflect the administration's change in attitude, not just as a positive change towards built heritage conservation, but also as a negative change against indigenous residents of the New Territories, as previously the administration, both colonial and post-colonial, rarely confronted or acted against them (Figs. 8.1, 8.2, 8.3, 8.4, 8.5 and 8.6).

8.4 Private Built Heritage Protection and Public Private Partnerships 101

Fig. 8.2 Blue House Wan Chai (colour)

Fig. 8.3 Cenotaph

8.4 Private Built Heritage Protection and Public Private Partnerships

Fig. 8.4 Empire Theatre (State Theatre) North Point

Fig. 8.5 Pagoda Ping Shan trail

Fig. 8.6 Leung Yeuk Tau Trail

References

1. Antiquities Advisory Board, Historic Building Appraisal N262, December 2016. Building Remains at Cochrane Street and Gutzlaff Street, Central, Hong Kong. https://www.aab.gov.hk/form/news_20161209/historic_3_new_items.pdf. Accessed 10 June 2021
2. Antiquities Advisory Board, Historic Building Appraisal N46, December 2016. Former State Theatre, J/O King's Road and Tin Chong Street, North Point, H.K. https://www.aab.gov.hk/form/news_20161209/historic_3_new_items.pdf. Accessed 10 June 2021
3. Antiquities Advisory Board. 1,444 historic buildings and new items in addition to 1,444 historic buildings—definition of the gradings. https://www.aab.gov.hk/en/built3.php. Accessed 10 June 2021
4. Antiquities Advisory Board. 1,444 historic buildings and new items in addition to 1,444 historic buildings—results of the assessment of 1,444 historic buildings. https://www.aab.gov.hk/en/aab.php. Accessed 10 June 2021
5. Antiquities Advisory Board (2014) Respecting our heritage while looking ahead: policy on conservation of built heritage consultation paper. https://www.gov.hk/en/residents/government/publication/consultation/docs/2014/CBH.pdf. Accessed 10 June 2021
6. Antiquities Advisory Board. Frequently asked questions on assessment of buildings in Hong Kong which may have heritage value. https://www.aab.gov.hk/form/AAB_brief_faq_en.pdf. Accessed 10 June 2021
7. Antiquities and Monuments office website: https://www.amo.gov.hk/en/monuments.php. Accessed 10 June 2021
8. Antiquities and Monuments Office. Assessment of 1,444 Historic Buildings. https://www.amo.gov.hk/en/built2.php. Accessed 10 June 2021
9. Antiquities and Monuments Office. Heritage Trails. Lung Yeuk Tau Heritage Trail http://www.amo.gov.hk/en/trails_lung.php. Accessed 10 June 2021
10. Antiquities and Monuments Office. Heritage Trails. Ping Shan Trail. http://www.amo.gov.hk/en/trails_pingshan.php. Accessed 10 June 2021

References

11. Broad Development Parameters of the Applied Use /Development in respect of Application No. A/SK-CWBN/4 Available via Hong Kong Government Information: https://www.info.gov.hk/tpb/tc/plan_application/Attachment/20180518/s16_A_SK-CWBN_48_0_gist.pdf. Accessed 10 June 2021
12. Central Market. http://www.centralmarket.hk/en/. Accessed 10 June 2021.
13. Chen J (2013) Ho Tung Gardens saga and the basis of compensation under the antiquities and monuments ordinance: a comparative and incentive case study on regulatory takings. Hong Kong L J 43:835
14. Chief Executive's Policy Address (2013) Seek change maintain stability serve the people with pragmatism: https://www.policyaddress.gov.hk/2013/eng/index.html. Accessed 10 June 2021
15. Conserve and Revitalise Hong Kong Heritage. Batch 1 of Revitalisation Scheme. https://www.heritage.gov.hk/en/rhbtp/ProgressResult_Tai_O_Police_Station.htm. Accessed 10 June 2021
16. Conserving Heritage—The Revitalisation of Tai Kwun. https://www.taikwun.hk/en/taikwun/heritage_conservation/restoration_timeline. Accessed 10 June 2021
17. Dewolf C. Zolimacitymag.com. 26 March 2020. Hong Kong's Colonial Heritage, Part III: 1881 Heritage The Malling of History. https://zolimacitymag.com/hong-kong-colonial-heritage-1881-heritage-malling-of-history/. Accessed 10 June 2021
18. Historical Laws of Hong Kong Online. http://oelawhk.lib.hku.hk/items/show/1219. Accessed 10 June 2021
19. Hong Kong Free Press. Sala I. 6 March, 201 Hong Kong's rare dragon kiln is under threat from a proposed housing development. https://www.hongkongfp.com/2018/03/06/hong-kongs-rare-dragon-kiln-threat-proposed-housing-development/. Accessed 10 June 2021
20. Hong Kong Police. Offbeat Online. Yau Ma Tei Police Station. https://www.police.gov.hk/offbeat/641/photo.html. Accessed 10 June 2021
21. K11. About the Chairman. https://hk.k11.com/about/. Accessed 10 June 2021
22. Kong Y (2013) The Inadequacy of Hong Kong's Conservation Legislation. Hong Kong Lawyer. http://www.hk-lawyer.org/content/inadequacy-hong-kongs-conservation-legislation. Accessed 10 June 2021
23. Lai A. Travel.Cnn.Com. 24 January 2013. What's the big deal about having a UNESCO World Heritage site? http://travel.cnn.com/hong-kong-world-heritage-site-020521/. Accessed 10 June 2021
24. Legislative Council Brief DEVB/CS/CR 4/1/83. February 200 Withdrawal of the Declaration of the Building at 128 Pok Fu Lam Road as a Proposed Monument. https://www.legco.gov.hk/yr07-08/english/subleg/brief/21_brf.pdf. Accessed 10 June 2021
25. Lord Wilson Heritage Trust. https://www.lordwilson-heritagetrust.org.hk/en/introduction/intro.html. Accessed 10 June 2021
26. Ma S (2010) Built heritage conservation and the voluntary sector: the case of the Tung Wah Coffin Home in Hong Kong. Int J Cult Prop 17:87–107
27. March 2009 publication of the assessment of 1,444 historic buildings: http://www.amo.gov.hk/en/built2.php. Accessed 10 June 2021
28. Meacham W (2015) The Struggle for Hong Kong's Heritage—narrative, documents and reminiscences of the early years. Published by the Author, Hong Kong
29. South China Morning Post, 06 April, 201 Letter- Hong Kong's post-war heritage building grading needs to be placed in the hands of specialists. http://www.scmp.com/comment/letters/article/2140512/hong-kongs-post-war-heritage-building-grading-needs-be-placed-hands. Accessed 10 June 2021
30. South China Morning Post. Xinqi S. South China Morning Post. 1 February 2019. Development of Hakka village in Hong Kong gets government approval despite fears over impact on surrounding area. https://www.scmp.com/news/hong-kong/hong-kong-economy/article/2184544/development-hakka-village-hong-kong-gets-government. Accessed 10 June 2021
31. South China Morning Post. 20 November 2012. Public denied access to Pok Fu Lam's Jessville mansion. https://www.scmp.com/news/hong-kong/article/1086296/public-denied-access-pok-fu-lams-jessville-mansion. Accessed 10 June 2021

32. South China Morning Post. Alex Lo. 22 November 2017. Central Market to serve up more disappointment. http://www.scmp.com/comment/insight-opinion/article/2120976/central-market-serve-more-disappointment. Accessed 10 June 2021
33. South China Morning Post. Cheung E. 22 October 201 Hopes rise for Hong Kong's historic State Theatre with developer New World aiming to save 'relevant part' of complex. https://www.scmp.com/news/hong-kong/society/article/2169721/hopes-rise-hong-kongs-historic-state-theatre-developer-new. Accessed 10 June 2021
34. South China Morning Post. Franchineau H. 20 January 2013. Victoria Harbour snubbed over nomination for World Heritage site status. https://www.scmp.com/news/hong-kong/article/1131920/victoria-harbour-snubbed-over-nomination-world-heritage-site-status. Accessed 10 June 2021
35. South China Morning Post. Fung F. 05 June, 2015. Hong Kong antiquities advisers hold heated debate over grading for Shaw Studios buildings. http://www.scmp.com/news/hong-kong/health-environment/article/1816778/hong-kong-antiquities-advisers-hold-heated-debate. Accessed 10 June 2021
36. South China Morning Post. Fung F. 4 June 2015. Just one building in Hong Kong's Shaw Studios proposed for top heritage grading. https://www.scmp.com/news/hong-kong/education-community/article/1816052/just-one-building-hong-kongs-shaw-studios. Accessed 10 June 2021
37. South China Morning Post. Ho P. 28 March, 201 Post-war buildings deserve a place in Hong Kong's architectural history. http://www.scmp.com/comment/insight-opinion/article/2139216/post-war-buildings-deserve-place-hong-kongs-architectural. Accessed 10 June 2021
38. South China Morning Post. Ng. J. 26 January 2011. Gardens a Living Reminder of our Colonial Past, Says Historians. https://www.scmp.com/article/736741/gardens-living-reminder-our-colonial-past-say-historians. Accessed 10 June 2021
39. South China Morning Post. Ng. J. 26 January 2011. Ho Tung Mansion Saved from Demolition. https://www.scmp.com/article/736742/ho-tung-mansion-saved-demolition. Accessed 10 June 2021
40. South China Morning Post. Kao E, Ng N. 7 November, 2017. Lai Chi Wo village chief insists on go-ahead for revitalisation plan despite opposing homeowners. http://www.scmp.com/news/hong-kong/health-environment/article/2118791/lai-chi-wo-village-chief-insists-go-ahead. Accessed 10 June 2021
41. South China Morning Post. Kao E. 9 March, 2017. Windows ripped out of Hong Kong's historic Red House despite ongoing preservation talks. http://www.scmp.com/news/hong-kong/education-community/article/2077174/windows-ripped-out-hong-kongs-historic-red-house. Accessed 10 June 2021
42. South China Morning Post. Kao. E. 15 June, 2017. Landmark Hong Kong land swap deal is a win for environmental conservation. https://www.scmp.com/news/hong-kong/health-environment/article/2098559/landmark-hong-kong-land-swap-deal-win. Accessed 10 June 2021
43. South China Morning Post. Lam N. 1 April 2021. Tour offers residents a final show at Hong Kong's State Theatre before heritage revamp. https://www.scmp.com/news/hong-kong/society/article/3128010/tour-offers-residents-final-show-hong-kongs-state-theatre. Accessed 10 June 2021
44. South China Morning Post. Leung C. 31 January, 2017. Era of reel and real life crime-fighting ends as Hong Kong bids farewell to iconic Yau Ma Tei police station. http://www.scmp.com/news/hong-kong/law-crime/article/2066478/era-reel-and-real-life-crime-fighting-ends-hong-kong-bids. Accessed 10 June 2021
45. South China Morning Post. Leung S. 8 December 2016. Victory for heritage activists as North Point's State Theatre to be awarded top protection grading. https://www.hongkongfp.com/2016/12/08/victory-for-heritage-activists-as-north-points-state-theatre-to-be-awarded-top-protection-grading/. Accessed 10 June 2021
46. South China Morning Post. Li S. 25 August 2020. Hong Kong's iconic State Theatre to be preserved under New World's multibillion-dollar redevelopment plan. https://www.scmp.com/business/article/3098710/hong-kongs-iconic-state-theatre-be-preserved-under-new-worlds-multibillion. Accessed 10 June 2021

47. South China Morning Post. Ng J. 18 December 2012. Shock over plans to make 14-year-old nunnery a UNESCO world heritage site. https://www.scmp.com/news/hong-kong/article/1107158/shock-over-plans-make-14-year-old-nunnery-unesco-world-heritage-site. Accessed 10 June 2021
48. South China Morning Post. Ng K, Ng N. 17 February, 2017. Hong Kong lawmaker seeks to buy time to prevent demolition of historic Red House in Tuen Mun. https://www.scmp.com/news/hong-kong/education-community/article/2071751/fears-historic-red-house-tuen-mun-may-be. Accessed 10 June 2021
49. South China Morning Post. Ng N. 1 November, 2017. Hong Kong's historic Blue House wins Unesco's highest heritage conservation award. http://www.scmp.com/news/hong-kong/community/article/2117982/hong-kongs-historic-blue-house-wins-unescos-highest. Accessed 10 June 2021
50. South China Morning Post. Ng N. 12 March 2017. Urban Renewal Authority pledges to consider preserving remains of 100-year-old buildings site. http://www.scmp.com/news/hong-kong/economy/article/2078221/urban-renewal-authority-pledges-consider-preserving-remains. Accessed 10 June 2021
51. South China Morning Post. Ng N. 13 March 2017. Structural safety to determine whether 19th century Hong Kong housing remains are preserved. http://www.scmp.com/news/hong-kong/education-community/article/2078439/structural-safety-determine-whether-19th-century. Accessed 10 June 2021
52. South China Morning Post. Singh H. 10 September, 2016. Hong Kong police station 'shows how city should preserve its heritage'. http://www.scmp.com/news/hong-kong/education-community/article/2018257/hong-kong-police-station-shows-how-city-should. Accessed 10 June 2021
53. South China Morning Post. Vetter D. 2 February 2019. How campaigners helped save Hong Kong's unique post-war State Theatre from wrecker's ball—and why majority owner New World Development had a rethink. https://www.scmp.com/news/hong-kong/society/article/2184551/how-campaigners-helped-save-hong-kongs-unique-post-war-state. Accessed 10 June 2021
54. South China Morning Post. Xinqi S. 11 December, 2017. Hong Kong conservationists urge rule change to save historic theatre.http://www.scmp.com/news/hong-kong/community/article/2123730/hong-kong-conservationists-urge-rule-change-save-historic. Accessed 10 June 2021
55. South China Morning Post. Xinqi S. 7 March, 201 Hongkongers fight to save city's only complete dragon kiln. http://www.scmp.com/news/hong-kong/community/article/2136049/hongkongers-fight-save-citys-only-complete-dragon-kiln. Accessed 10 June 2021
56. South China Morning Post. Yiu E. 29 August, 2017. Return to its glorious past for Hong Kong's old Bank of China building in Central. http://www.scmp.com/property/hong-kong-china/article/2108720/return-its-glorious-past-hong-kongs-old-bank-china-building. Accessed 10 June 2021
57. South China Morning Post. Zhao S. 1 April, 201 Historic Hong Kong police compound's mystery 'Rehearsal' as future arts hub. http://www.scmp.com/print/news/hong-kong/community/article/2139764/historic-hong-kong-police-compounds-mystery-rehearsal. Accessed 10 June 2021
58. South China Morning Post. Zhao S. 25 March, 201 Historic Hong Kong police compound to partially reopen as heritage and arts centre in May. http://www.scmp.com/news/hong-kong/community/article/2138806/historic-hong-kong-police-compound-partially-reopen. Accessed 10 June 2021
59. South China Morning Post. Zhao S. 25 March, 201 Residents fear huge influx of visitors when historic Hong Kong police station compound reopens. http://www.scmp.com/news/hong-kong/community/article/2138811/residents-fear-huge-influx-visitors-when-historic-hong-kong. Accessed 10 June 2021
60. South China Morning Post. Zhao S. 26 October, 2017. Historic Hong Kong Red House set to be preserved for 10 years. http://www.scmp.com/news/hong-kong/health-environment/article/2117076/historic-hong-kong-red-house-set-be-preserved-10. Accessed 10 June 2021

61. South China Morning Post. Zhao S. 8 March, 2017. Hong Kong hospital tears down historic arch to make way for barrier-free access. http://www.scmp.com/news/hong-kong/education-community/article/2077140/hong-kong-hospital-tears-down-historic-arch-make. Accessed 10 June 2021
62. Tai O Heritage Hotel website: http://www.taioheritagehotel.com/en/. Accessed 10 June 2021
63. UNESCO World Heritage List. The Criteria for Selection. http://whc.unesco.org/en/criteria/. Accessed 10 June 2021
64. UNESCO World Heritage Sites. Historic Centre of Macao. https://whc.unesco.org/en/list/1110/. Accessed 10 June 2021
65. UNESCO. The World Heritage List. https://whc.unesco.org/en/list/. Accessed 10 June 2021
66. Urban Renewal Authority. Heritage Preservation & Revitalisation. Mallory Street / Burrows Street. https://www.ura.org.hk/en/project/heritage-preservation-and-revitalisation/mallory-street-burrows-street. Accessed 10 June 2021
67. Urban Renewal Authority. Heritage Preservation & Revitalisation. Central Market. https://www.ura.org.hk/en/project/heritage-preservation-and-revitalisation/central-market Accessed 10 June 2021.
68. Urban Renewal Authority. Redevelopment. Nga Tsin Wai Village Project (K1). https://www.ura.org.hk/en/project/redevelopment/nga-tsin-wai-village-project. Accessed 10 June 2021
69. Wordie J (2002) Streets: exploring Hong Kong island. Hong Kong University Press, Hong Kong, pp 74–75
70. World Economic Forum. 3 December 2020. These are the countries with the most UNESCO World Heritage sites. https://www.weforum.org/agenda/2020/12/unesco-world-heritage-countries-history-archaeology-landmarks-italy-china/. Accessed 10 June 2021
71. Yeung, Hester Au (2012) Heritage in Hong Kong-city with/without history. Journal of the Departmefnt of Planning and Architecture UWE: 58–61. https://www2.uwe.ac.uk/faculties/FET/news/publications/Project2012.pdf. Accessed 10 June 2021

Chapter 9
Conclusions and The Future for Built Heritage Protection in Hong Kong

Abstract Hong Kong's record of built heritage protection evidences many failures and significant losses under the colonial and post-colonial governments. However, Hong Kong retains important evidence of its history in the form of significant built heritage. That built heritage is subject to limited protection under the legal and regulatory system. Popular action has been and continues to be the most effective factor in the development of the protection of built heritage in Hong Kong.

The protection of built heritage in Hong Kong was criticised before and has been criticised since the implementation of the Antiquities and Monuments Ordinance in 1976. Both the colonial and post-colonial governments have been criticised, often justifiably, as regarding Hong Kong's built heritage as irrelevant in the face of the pressing need for living space in this small region. The Antiquities and Monuments Ordinance remains the only statute providing limited protection for Hong Kong's identified built heritage if it meets the specification of an antiquity or is designated as a monument. However, under the post-colonial government there has proved a more important factor in protecting built heritage than any law—the power of public opinion. That opinion did not sway the colonial government in its decisions with regard to built heritage, as evidenced by the demolition of the KCR station at Tsim Shat Tsui, the Old Hong Kong Club building and the retreat from protection of the Ohel Leah Synagogue. However, it is notable that in and after 2007, concessions were made when the public made clear their displeasure at the loss of built heritage, although not always a concession to save the disputed heritage. The introduction of new policies, new initiatives and a commitment to honouring these, has meant that Hong Kong's built heritage has a better chance of survival today. That does not mean that these policies have not failed at times, and that there have not been questions about government decisions, mistakes and apathy.

There is much room for improvement for the policy and law intended to protect built heritage in Hong Kong. This is not limited to the recommendations of the 2014 Consultation. Simple measures such as revisiting the Antiquities and Monuments Ordinance itself and, considering it was originally intended to protect archaeological finds, introducing a stand-alone statute for built heritage protection. This new statute could include the Antiquities Advisory Board's Grading system as an initial means of statutory protection. Apart from this, a true commitment to the implementation of heritage impact assessments could justify the unwarranted praise that has been accorded this policy.

In spite of the need of reform of the legal and regulatory protective framework for built heritage and the fact that Hong Kong has lost important elements of its built heritage in colonial and post-colonial times, the future seems quite positive for Hong Kong's built heritage. This is because of the people of Hong Kong and the government's surprising respect for public opinion on this subject. Many Hong Kongers have committed themselves, financially or through their work as volunteers and activists to promote the celebration and protection of Hong Kong's built heritage. Perhaps most importantly recently, many have utilised social media to protest and lobby the government, and the government has responded positively.[1] As an example of the importance of built heritage to the people of Hong Kong, the impact of social media and the government's acceptance of this importance and respect for it, there is the recently publicised case of the Bishop's Hill "Water Cathedral".

In late 2020, news broke that a 100-year-old water cistern or reservoir in the Bishop's Hill area of Kowloon was being demolished by government workers. The story circulated because photographs of the inside of the cistern and the first stages of demolition were published on social media and went viral. The photographs showed elegant stone arches reminiscent of a Roman palace or a gothic cathedral, which earned the cistern the nickname, the "Water Cathedral".[2] Immediately, there was criticism that this seemingly unknown gem of Hong Kong's built heritage was being demolished. The government immediately ordered the demolition to cease and announced very shortly afterwards that the building would be preserved.[3] The Commissioner for Heritage, Ivanhoe Chang, made a public apology for insensitivity and miscommunication among staff and government engineers over the demolition work.[4] The Antiquities Advisory Board apologised for not having brought this building to public notice before. A few days later, the Water Supplies Department (WSD) and the Antiquities and Monuments Office confirmed reports that the service reservoir at Hatton Road in Mid-Levels, dating back to 1908, was knocked down nine years before with the consent of heritage officials.[5] In June, the Antiquities Advisory board backed grade 1 status for three similar reservoirs.[6] Such admissions and reactions epitomise the government's surprisingly meek and appeasing attitude when faced with protests over heritage. These are not the usual reactions Hong Kong governments have had to public criticism or protests—in the past or recently. However, with heritage issues, for some reason, perhaps the memories of the demonstrations of 2006 and 2007, any issue involving built heritage does seem to get a positive reaction from the government and people of Hong Kong. Of course, it

---

[1] Kong Free Press [2].
[2] Dimsum daily [1].
[3] South China Morning Post [3].
[4] South China Morning Post [4].
[5] South China Morning Post [5].
[6] South China Morning Post [6].

9 Conclusions and The Future for Built Heritage Protection … 111

could just be members of the Hong Kong government appreciate Hong Kong's built heritage themselves.

The strength of public commitment to protecting the built heritage of Hong Kong has noticeably developed since the return of Hong Kong to China. This may be linked to a number of factors, but foremost is the idea that the majority of people in Hong Kong want Hong Kong to retain its identify as a special place within and as part of China. Thus, they do not want to see any aspect of their history and heritage destroyed.[7] Whatever the reasons, public support for the protection of built heritage and the government's recognition of and respect for this support means that the future for Hong Kong's built heritage- pre-colonial, colonial and post-colonial- looks far brighter than it has done before in Hong Kong's history.

References

1. Dimsum daily (2020) Century-old Roman-style underground cistern uncovered on Bishop Hill in Shek Kip Mei. https://www.dimsumdaily.hk/100-year-old-roman-structure-discovered-at-top-reservoir-of-bishop-hill-in-shek-kip-mei/. Accessed 10 June 2021
2. Hong Kong Free Press, Lai C (2021) Timespan: iconic arches represent a rare victory for Hong Kong's heritage campaigners. https://hongkongfp.com/2021/05/09/timespan-iconic-arches-represent-a-rare-victory-for-hong-kongs-heritage-campaigners/. Accessed 15 June 2021
3. South China Morning Post, Leung C (2021) Century-old reservoir in Hong Kong's Bishop Hill proposed to be made a grade one historic building. https://www.scmp.com/news/hong-kong/society/article/3124298/century-old-reservoir-hong-kongs-bishop-hill-proposed-be. Accessed 10 June 2021
4. South China Morning Post, Ng J, Yeo R (2020) Head of Hong Kong heritage office sorry for 'insensitivity' over plan to demolish striking century-old site, but unanswered questions fuel backlash. https://www.scmp.com/news/hong-kong/society/article/3115703/head-hong-kong-heritage-office-apologises-insensitivity-over. Accessed 11 June 2021
5. South China Morning Post, Yeo R (2021) Panel backs grade one heritage status for three of Hong Kong's century-old reservoirs.https://www.scmp.com/news/hong-kong/society/article/3136837/hong-kong-panel-backs-grade-one-heritage-status-three. Accessed 15 June 2021
6. South China Morning Post, Yeo R (2021) With heritage preservation in the spotlight, Hong Kong authorities reveal century-old structure was demolished nine years ago: https://www.scmp.com/news/hong-kong/society/article/3116848/heritage-preservation-spotlight-hong-kong-authorities-reveal. Accessed 11 June 2021
7. Yung E, Chan E (2011) Problem issues of public participation in built-heritage conservation: two controversial cases in Hong Kong. Habitat Int 35:457–466

---

[7] See the conclusions of Yung and Chan [7], 457.

Printed in the United States
by Baker & Taylor Publisher Services